Adventures in Belief

ADVENTURES
in BELIEF

*How I Discovered the Meaning of Life,
the Universe, and Everything (Possibly)*

Keith Ward

CASCADE *Books* • Eugene, Oregon

Cascade Books
An Imprint of Wipf and Stock Publishers
199 W. 8th Ave., Suite 3
Eugene, OR 97401

www.wipfandstock.com

PAPERBACK ISBN: 978–1-6667–5623–4
HARDCOVER ISBN: 978–1-6667–5624–1
EBOOK ISBN: 978–1-6667–5625–8

Cataloguing-in-Publication data:

Names: Ward, Keith, 1938– [author].

Title: Adventures in belief : how I discovered the meaning of life, the universe, and everything (possibly) / Keith Ward.

Description: Eugene, OR: Cascade Books, 2022

Identifiers: ISBN 978–1-6667–5623–4 (paperback) | ISBN 978–1-6667–5624–1 (hardcover) | ISBN 978–1-6667–5625–8 (ebook)

Subjects: LCSH: Autobiographies | Intellectual development | Religion and science | Christian philosophy | Christianity and other religions | Career development

Classification: BT75.3 W37 2022 (print) | BT75.3 (ebook)

VERSION NUMBER 122922

To my wife, Marian, and my two children, Fiona and Alun

CONTENTS

MAP

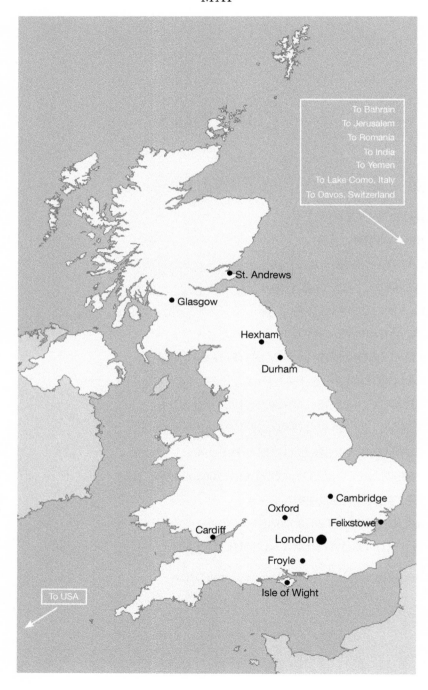

INTRODUCTION

I have been in two minds about writing this book. One mind is a mind that takes the ordinary events of life with a dash of good humour and sees the funny side even of things that are not obviously funny to anyone else. The other mind is a mind that cannot stop thinking about ultimate human questions like, Is there a deep meaning to human existence? or, Could everything really be just an accident? I am not sure it is possible to combine these two minds—I know many people who cannot. But they do exist in me, and they have produced a particular way of seeing life that has proved very fulfilling, so I thought that might be worth passing on.

It is also the case that thoughts, even very abstract thoughts like mine, do not just exist in a vacuum. They have a local habitation and a name, and they arise in a very specific historical and cultural situation. This means they have many limitations of their time and place, but also attempt to tackle various problems of that time in a positive and personal way. The perspective they express is a blend of insights and oversights, and I thought it might explain to my children what on earth their father has been doing all these years, when I could have had, as my own father might have put it, 'a proper job' in 'the real world.'

So this is a short story of my life and thought, and how I came to a form of belief that I call *personal idealism*. It is primarily a story about the development of ideas and beliefs, and that is its central focus. As such, it is most likely to appeal to those who are interested in philosophical questions, or at least would like to know something about how some contemporary philosophical ideas have developed. But such developments are always shaped by the places and cultures in which one has lived, and the things that one has done. I have lived through a time of tragic wars, revolutions, viral pandemics, and the growth of new military dictatorships in the world. But it has also been a time of great scientific discoveries, flights to the moon, the decoding of DNA, and the invention of computers. There has been enormous change, and our world is both in real danger of complete destruction and yet capable as never before of generating great advances in global understanding and in human health and well-being. It is no exaggeration to say that our world is precariously poised between self-destruction and the possibility of a new age of personal fulfilment.

My philosophy has been influenced by the realisation that most individuals can do little about these great issues of our time, yet that the human future depends on building social structures and personal attitudes that may increase empathetic understanding, positive creativity, and genuine concern for the welfare of others. It is in such things that hope for the future lies, and every person can do something to realise them in their own lives, however seemingly insignificant they may appear to be.

My own small part has been played out in the privileged environment of liberal English-speaking university life. But I have also been affected by the fears and hopes that the events of my time have generated. This has resulted in a philosophy that stresses personal moral responsibility, hope for the future, but also acceptance of the ever-present self-destructive possibilities, the frailties, greed, and hatreds that are seemingly inherent in human nature. Trying to hold these things together led in my case to the philosophy of personal idealism.

My form of personal idealism is Christian, though it can and does exist in other religious traditions and none. I think that it forms a basis for fellowship with many like-thinking people in many different cultures and faiths throughout the world, though I may be unduly optimistic about this. At least one of my minds is unduly optimistic anyway, though the other one always adds a degree of scepticism. I do not suppose I will ever know which is nearer to truth.

BEGINNINGS

A NORTHUMBRIAN CHILDHOOD

In 1938 two events of great importance to me happened. Germany annexed Austria and Sudetenland, foreshadowing the outbreak of the Second World War, and I was born. In the great scheme of things, the former was obviously the more important, but the latter was of decisive importance to me and my mother. I think that I was born prematurely, but I confess that I cannot remember very clearly.

A philosophical baby (1938)

My earliest life was expedited during wartime, but I am almost embarrassed to say that I found it most enjoyable. I apologise if this sounds dismissive of the real tragedies of war, but I have to say that, by luck, none of those tragedies touched my young and innocent life. Of course, I had no idea of what was really going. But it meant that my father joined the Royal Air Force, leaving me in sole possession of my mother, which was greatly to my satisfaction. She had five sisters, who all lived in the same house, Dene House, which was my maternal grandfather's house, so I was in effect brought up by six women, who all gave me their sweet rations (sweets were severely rationed during the war). That was even more greatly to my satisfaction.

Although my father was later posted overseas, he at first spent time on the Isle of Wight and in Felixstowe. Most people from these places were evacuated to safer parts of the country. My mother, being of a very independent mind, went to live in these 'dangerous' places, to be near my father. One advantage of this was that we lived in large and luxurious houses, since their owners had fled, and though we did experience a few bombs, on the whole I enjoyed watching dogfights in the air, and the general feeling of, as it seemed to me, excitement and adventure. This may sound terrible, but at that time I had no idea of the horrors of war, and what I dimly remember is what seemed like a number of games in which planes fought in a distant sky, and bombers droned overhead in impressive numbers on their way to places far away. None of it seemed to threaten serious harm to me. Such was the innocence and ignorance of childhood.

One of the few things I remember clearly is that when my father eventually returned from his overseas posting, I asked my mother, "When is that man going to leave?" This was not a good start to later relations with my father. Though he did his best for me, I always had the suspicion that he was an interloper, and we spent most of the next few years shouting at one another.

When the war was over, we returned to our little hometown of Hexham, in Northumberland, a beautiful and very rural part of England bordering Scotland, a land of fells, moors, and heather, where there was nothing much to do but watch Hadrian's Wall being rebuilt so that it looked more like a truly impressive monument, and count sheep, which were all over the place. My grandfather had a farm (really, a house with a few fields, and some cows, hens, geese, and mice). It was called Dene House, and though it was quite large, having room for seven children and two adults, it had no bathroom or inside lavatory. When I stayed there, I had baths in a large tin bath by the open fire, and hot water was brought in by hand—it seemed very luxurious at the time. Going to the lavatory was quite a smelly experience, and required going 'around the corner' to an outhouse with a wooden bench with a hole in it. Some farmhouses had a 'double netty,' a bench with two holes next to each other, so that users could continue their conversations in peace. We, however, were spared that opportunity! I spent much time there (not in the outhouse, but in the fields), being chased by the cows, pecked by the geese, ignored by the hens, and infested by the mice.

I remember it as an idyllic childhood. Both my father and my mother were members of large families, and I was the eldest of many cousins, and had lots of aunts and uncles. So, though I was an only child, and so very spoilt, I experienced an extensive family life, filled with parties and all sorts of social events. I know that some unpleasant things must have happened, but they have receded in my mind to a place beyond my feelings. What I remember and still feel is the friendly buzzing of bees in sunny fields (in my memory, it was always sunny, though I realise that cannot be true), and the annual loading of mown hay with pitchforks into horse-drawn carts, on which we rode to neighbouring farms. The horses were happy, the bees were happy, everyone, it seemed, was happy.

I do dimly recall that I ran away from home on a number of occasions. I do not remember why, but I expect it was to do with arguments with my father. I really was a very mischievous and naughty child, and as he had a very short temper, I must have driven him mad. Anyway, I only ran to Dene House, which was four miles away, and I always returned after a day or so.

Back in the town, on the way to my school I played complex games of traversing from one side of the cattle mart to the other without touching the ground, just using the iron railings of the cattle stalls. I slid rapidly, and illegally, down spiralling chutes, which were meant to convey grain from the top to the bottom floor of the grain mill. And I played tennis and badminton for what seemed like most of the rest of the time. My memory tells me that I enjoyed school too, sitting in eternally sunlit classrooms with caring and attentive teachers, writing little plays, singing beautiful songs, and making little models out of plasticine. My memory may be better than the reality, but it is none the worse for that.

When I was tired of jumping, sliding, and hitting balls, of counting sheep and fleeing from cows, I read books. My grandmother used to say, "Are you reading those boring old books again?" And I always was. I read

5

everything I could get my hands on. In those days, Boots the Chemist had libraries. You could go in and get a bottle of cough medicine and read a volume of the *Children's Encyclopaedia* (for about sixpence a week).

The books I read were often very peculiar. Many of them were about religion, since Boots seemed to attract people who wanted to know if the afterlife would be less boring than this one. Also, the countryside around where we lived was filled with Methodist chapels. They have now all turned into desirable country residences, but then every tiny village or hamlet used to have a Methodist chapel. In fact, many of them had two chapels, because Methodists could never agree with each other. There was often a Wesleyan chapel and a Primitive Methodist chapel. I do not recall what the difference was, but I did not like the sound of being 'primitive,' so I suppose I was Wesleyan. The main difference in fact was that they virtually belonged to different families, which did not speak to one another, for reasons that nobody could remember.

The chapel at one end of the hamlet where my mother's parents lived was apparently run by my grandmother (who played the organ) and her friends (who gossiped, criticised each other's hats, and chewed sweets noisily during the sermon). That was not surprising, because the sermons were also given by various friends of my grandmother. They might have been very interesting, though they mostly seemed to be about the dreadful things that were happening on the farms next to theirs, and they could not be heard very well, because of the noise of sweet-chewing.

I do remember one prayer (people stood up to pray when they felt inspired, though I recall one venerable lady saying to her husband, "Sit down, John, you are not inspired") that went like this; "Thou knowest, O Lord, who sold me that cow. And Thou knowest, Lord, that the cow died." I do not remember what he went on to tell the Lord, but there was some very uncomfortable shuffling going on in the seat behind me.

Religious observance was very pleasant, if sometimes rather boring. There were lovely teas, plenty of people to play with, lots of intriguing gossip, even if I did not know what it was about, and many funny hats (as it seemed to me). Also, the books I read fascinated me. You may think that in a small rural town in the North of England things would be conventional and routine. Perhaps they were; but the books opened up vistas of fantasy and exotic experience.

THE SECRETS OF THE UNIVERSE

As I say, for some reason, there was a large section in Boots of books about theosophy and occultism—perhaps this was a sort of alternative therapy, and cheaper than bottles of Carter's Little Liver Pills. By the time I was ten, I had access to the deepest secrets of the universe, which were apparently to be found in the works of Rudolf Steiner and Annie Besant.

Strangely enough, one of my Methodist Sunday School teachers was a theosophist, a follower of the secret doctrines of Steiner and Besant—a fact that had probably escaped the attention of the Methodist authorities. Week by week, he told us about angels and archangels, dominions, powers, cherubim and seraphim, and the spiritual world from which we had all descended into matter, so that we could do the important 'work' of getting back to where we had originally come from.

It was very hard to distinguish all this from science fiction, which I much enjoyed. As soon as I had collected enough pocket money, I joined an American group called the Rosicrucians (AMORC). They were allegedly a secret fellowship of enlightened minds who had knowledge of the spiritual nature of the universe, knowledge that had been hidden for generations, though it had apparently been well known to the people of Atlantis and ancient Egypt, and could only be revealed to initiates. For a small fee, you could embark on a course that would reveal the secrets of the Great Pyramids, restore your hair if you were bald, and tell you the meaning of life.

I stayed with them for a number of years. However, I found that to attain the higher grades of initiation, more money was required than I had. The meaning of life was more expensive than I had expected, and I had to postpone my search.

There was, however, a less expensive religious influence in my early life. As a boy, I had quite a good voice, and so for some years I became a chorister in Hexham Abbey choir. This meant walking up and down some ancient stairs in the Abbey—which was a very large and historically significant, originally Saxon, church—singing a lot, and actually being *paid* for it. Being more or less a Methodist, even if I was a Rosicrucian one, I was at first rather shocked to get paid for going to church. But I got over that, though I never fully associated singing in the choir with religion. The services were a complete mystery to me; I could not understand why people kept standing up and kneeling down at various points, the sermons were inaudible, and the Psalms were incomprehensible. I loved the music, though. However, there is no doubt that the Methodists had a better badminton court, and a better table tennis table too. So, they won on points.

MUSIC

There is little doubt that religion played quite a large part in my early life. My parents did not practice any religion. I think my mother had heard too many Methodist local preachers in her youth, and the only religion my father respected was the Salvation Army, which at least showed practical concern for people in poverty. He was always a very generous man, a 'soft touch' for a sob story, and was the welfare officer for the local branch of the Royal Air Force association. My solitary reading was very eclectic, so the beliefs I was exposed to were not confined to any one orthodox system, and were often distinctly odd and what one might call 'new age.' The thing that I loved more than anything else was music, and I think the nearest thing I had to religious experiences were conveyed by music, which seemed to me to communicate some apprehension of beauty and also of an underlying mood of sadness that could not be conveyed in words, but revealed something important about the nature of human experience.

My father was an excellent musician. He could play a wide range of instruments, the saxophone being his favourite, and he even had his own band, which played for local dances and parties, as well as playing in the brass bands that were very popular in our part of the country. Despite the fact that we had a fairly stormy relationship—every conversation we had seemed to end in a shouting match—he was basically a kind and caring father, and was very concerned to foster my love of music. He went with me to music appreciation classes, and shut me in our small sitting room with our little upright piano for an hour every day, the result of which was that I shot through the grades of the Associated Board of Music, finishing them all (with distinction, I have to say) before I left school.

I was pretty good by Hexham standards, picking up lots of trophies from local musical festivals, and I was quite pleased with myself. It was not until later that I found out that Hexham was quite a small place, and the world beyond was full of pianists who were better than I was. I learned my first lesson in life: there is always somebody better than you (unless you happen to be Jesus, of course, and possibly Mozart—oh, and Bach too).

GRAMMAR SCHOOL LIFE

Because I was good at reading and at music, I passed the 'eleven-plus' examination. This was a test, which used to exist in those days, given to state school children at the age of eleven, for deciding who was respectable and expected to do well in life (to be an accountant or at least work in an office), and separating them from those who were more disreputable and would not get a decent office job (though they might well become millionaires, they would never really be middle-class). The ones who passed went to the local grammar school—the Queen Elizabeth Grammar School for boys. That was the first Queen Elizabeth, and it was quite an old school. It had some pretensions to being a public school (in England, that means a fee-paying boarding school); it was divided into 'houses,' which had Latin mottos, uniforms, and badges; and the pupils played rugby, as opposed to football. These were small signs of class distinction, though they fooled no one who had ever been to a real public school, and looked down on grammar schools with a sense of effortless superiority. Although it was a day school, it had a boarding house, because many pupils lived on far-flung farms, from which it was not possible to travel every day. There were only 180 boys in the school, so it was a small and cohesive community, and had the advantage of being next to a girl's school, which helped to provide entertainment for the older boys. A moment of choice came later, when the school had to decide whether to become independent (fee-paying) or comprehensive, and it chose the latter. At that point, the Queen Elizabeth Grammar School ceased to exist, and one more prop of the English class system was removed.

Social class was an important feature of life in those days (the 1940s). In Hexham, at the bottom was the 'sink estate,' a big estate of council houses, available for very low rents, where all the naughty boys and girls lived. Then, at the other end of town, was another council estate for the respectable working classes. My paternal grandmother lived there. Because she had a big family, it was a big house with a big garden, and naturally it was very respectable. My grandfather looked after the furnace in a small factory in town and made me little lead soldiers for Christmas in his furnace. The story was that he had come down in the world because of a fondness for alcohol, but when I knew him, he was quite reformed and respectable. I spent some time living with them, too, especially during the war, and much enjoyed it, as I was allowed to do things that my parents would have disapproved of, like listening to the radio late at night. It is hard to remember that there were no televisions then, and telephones were scarce and threatening. They were threatening because they only seemed to ring when there was bad news, like somebody dying. Few people had phones of their own, and you had to go to a little red public telephone box and insert some pennies into a slot before you could make a phone call. I actually got a badge in the Boy Scouts for being able to use a telephone. No wonder people of my age have trouble in adapting to mobile phones, which enable people to talk to almost anyone at any time for no reason at all, and cause them continually to collide with people as they walk along the street, talking loudly to invisible friends.

Our house in Hexham was a traditional red-brick, two-up, two-down, terrace house. My parents considered it quite superior, because it was the first house in the terrace to have a bathroom. The terrace was also next to the County Cricket Ground, so it was very quiet, though cricket balls did keep landing in the garden from time to time. We never moved from that house, largely because the rent always remained at fifteen shillings a week—that is 75p in modern money (equivalent to about £27 in 2022), which was quite a bargain, I suppose.

The house placed us on the boundary between the respectable working class and the lower middle class. That was because my father started life as a commercial traveller for a big drapery company. He drove around all the remote farms in Northumberland selling clothes and so on to the farmer's wives. That put him, I suppose, in the respectable working class. Then he went into business for himself, and so became, in his words, a master draper. This was definitely middle class, but only just, and my father liked driving around Northumberland so much that he always refused to move anywhere else, despite opportunities to do so. He actually had one of the first 'hire purchase' businesses in the area—where you could buy things on credit, and pay for them week by week. But he was so soft-hearted that he let people build up quite large unpaid debts. He also, sadly, lost enthusiasm when he found that I had no interest in ladies' underwear or in building up a large drapery business. He consequently decided just to make enough to live on and to keep on driving around Northumberland for the rest of his life.

My mother was very intelligent, but had been made to leave school at eleven, so that she could help to look after all the babies that were being born at Dene House. She became a quite excellent baker, and my school friends competed for invitations to tea at our house. My father and I practically lived on chocolate eclairs, Victoria sponges, layer cakes, apple tarts, and rock buns, until at last my father died eating a cream cake. It has always seemed to me an enviable death, though it did upset the other people who were there. After that my mother continued to operate the well-loved little drapers' shop in Hexham herself, and she was eventually rewarded, some years later, by seeing me obtain what she thought of as 'a good position,' which she could casually mention to everyone she met.

When I went to the grammar school, I became more solidly middle class, mixing with the children of farmers, accountants, and solicitors, who provided the grammar school with most of its children. My maternal grandfather probably fitted in here, since he had some cows, and owned his own butcher's business, in which the cows participated, not very enthusiastically. There were also a few upper-middle-class children, whose parents lived in large, detached houses but did not believe in public schools. Out of sight of most of us were the landed gentry, of whom there were a lot in Northumberland. I never met them, except when I worked as a waiter in a local hotel during school holidays, and served them coffee. Finally, above them were the aristocracy, who probably lived on a different planet, but occasionally descended to Hexham to observe the indigenous natives.

This system may seem peculiar, but everyone knew their place. Most people were very happy with their place, as long as it was higher than somebody else's place. Only the people in the sink estates did not feel superior to anybody, but they did not care about anybody, so they were happy too. Overall, it was a very happy place. Nobody realised how much things were going to change. As my mother used to say, "The trouble is, they are coming in from the South"—she meant, from Durham, the adjacent county just south of Northumberland, which was definitely, she thought, a county much less distinguished than Northumberland (even when the name of our county was changed to Northumbria, she refused to admit it).

I did not have a particularly distinguished career at the grammar school. Fortunately, my mother never found this out. When my school reports said, "He could not do any better," she thought this meant I was the best possible student. When my desk was moved to the front of the class so that teachers could keep their eye on me, she thought this was because I was top of the class. When I was put into Form 4X (that was a wooden hut in the school grounds for pupils who were so unruly that X was the only appropriate letter to give them), she thought the X was short for 'excellent.'

I did distinguish myself in some ways. I edited the school magazine; I played the piano for school assemblies; and I acted (usually as the leading lady, since the school was for boys only) in school plays. But on the whole, I was the despair of teachers, who thought I should be working hard on the subjects I was supposed to be studying. What they did not notice was that I took care never to be very bottom of the class, doing just enough to avoid that fate.

The worst case was Latin, for which I had a particular dislike, thinking that a dead language was only useful for lawyers, Catholic priests, and other pretentious people. As a faithful Rosicrucian Methodist and Anglican chorister, I refused to learn Latin on principle. It turned out to be a particularly stupid principle, because university entry into any humanities subject in those days demanded a pass in Latin O-level. So, when the time came, I could not be accepted by any English university. All the same, in my last year in school, I did decide to work, and suddenly I actually won so many prizes that they had to give some of my prizes to other people. When I came top in the A level and scholarship exams, which were the final school examinations, one of my teachers, who had watched my irritating lack of attention for many years, merely said, "You little bugger": and that just about sums up my school career.

THE ROYAL AIR FORCE

Anyway, because of my hatred of Latin, and my consequent inability to get into any university to study subjects I was interested in until I had passed a Latin examination, I then joined the Royal Air Force. To be more precise, I was 'called up' for National Service, which was rumoured to consist of two years of marching up and down, painting lumps of coal on camp roads white, and generally doing things that had no possible use in the rest of one's life.

Of the options available, the Air Force seemed to me the best bet, because they did not usually paint lumps of coal or run around with bayonets. I was duly accepted into the ranks, after an absurd interview with an officer who thought I was a hotel porter (as I sometimes was, during my holidays from school), and asked me if I really enjoyed carrying bags around. I said that I did, and he assigned me to be a clerk (Organisation branch), those being the people who carried most bags around. Also, clerks also had the fewest weeks to endure training camp, which I was keen to avoid, as there is a limit to what you have to know in order to carry bags around effectively.

At the training camp, we had to do all sorts of square-bashing and rifle drills, but fortunately I escaped most of those, because I was assigned to the Sports Flight. This was, like most of my life, due to a mistake. When asked what I had done at school, I said I had done a lot of cross-country running. I had, for a number of reasons. The countryside was beautiful. It was a good way of getting out of school. And I always arranged to drop into a nearby farm for a cup of coffee, re-joining the pack of other runners as they returned from their more strenuous exertions over the fells.

Thus it was that I found myself in a billet—a large oblong hut filled with the beds and kitbags and smells of about thirty bewildered people from other ranks, all of whom (except me) were tough athletes, boxers, body-builders, and gymnasts, who spent most of their time training and doing press-ups. Once again luck was with me, as I spent most of my time running off into the country around the camp, and having a rest where nobody could see me.

The time came, however, when I had to run for the RAF against the Army. To my surprise, I was not last. Someone called Gordon Pirie was first (he became a famous runner), and I was thirty-second, out of over a hundred runners. I thought this was pretty good, but I was never asked to run again, and I went back to learning how to carry bags properly, and also how to put files in the right order (that is, an order that nobody else could understand, so that I could retain full control of the filing system, and make myself indispensable).

On active service in Bahrain

A YEAR IN BAHRAIN

The RAF did not really know what to do with National Servicemen, who were only there for two years, and they asked me where I would like to be posted. I suggested a small RAF camp in Northumberland, rather near Hexham, preferably with very few planes around—they are unduly noisy at night, I find. The authorities listened kindly to what I said, and then I was sent to Bahrain, an island in what was then the Persian Gulf, thousands of miles away from Hexham and the nearest fish and chip shop.

I do not know what we were doing in Bahrain, and certainly nobody knew what I was supposed to be doing. It was too hot to carry many bags around, and at that time (it was 1956) the political situation was very complicated. Basically, the British thought they were in charge; the Arabs thought they were not; and the consequence was that we clerks spent our time sending out orders to the population, which the population promptly threw in the nearest bin. We were also, unusually for the Air Force, given rifles, but we were not allowed ammunition. If we were on guard duty, as we sometimes were, and came across a hostile tribesman, we were to say, "Halt, who goes there?" Then, if we received the reply, "I am a hostile Arab," we were supposed to say, "Excuse me for a moment, while I go and get some ammunition to shoot you with." Fortunately, I never had to see if this worked. In fact, I never had to confront any hostile Arabs, except the one who used to make tea for me. He would say, "This year I make tea for you. Next year you make tea for me," which I found vaguely threatening. But then he would defuse the situation by saying, "Would you like to meet my sister?" However, I suspected that was some sort of threat as well, so I never did. Some of my colleagues did, however, and reported back that the experience was quite pleasurable.

I worked in HQ, and the sergeant in charge of the office did not like National Servicemen. They lacked, he thought, the necessary professional competence to make it look as if they were working hard when there was very little to do. They also did not take their position seriously enough, and tended to giggle when they were given orders and made to stand to attention. For conduct of that sort, I was actually put on a 'charge' for two weeks, which meant that I had to put on a clean uniform, with mirror-shining shoes and sparkling buckles on my webbing, and 'buffer' some floor—that means pushing a heavy mop-like object on the end of a pole up and down a wooden floor until the floor gleamed like ice.

This was very difficult for me, since I spent a lot of time in the office cranking the handle of a Xerox duplicating machine—duplicating the orders that were destined to fill Arabic rubbish bins—which meant that all my uniforms were covered in blotches of duplicating ink. Also, all my buckles had discoloured in the heat. To cap it all, my uniform never had fit me very well, and my short trousers kept falling down. For all those reasons, I was not ever allowed to go on official parades with the rest of the troops. The last straw was that the 'buffer' which was supposed to buff the floor was too heavy for me to buff.

But there was a surprising salvation at hand. The military policeman whose floor I was supposed to buff—a muscular giant of a man whose shorts never fell down—found out that I played the piano. It was not actually a piano, which would never have survived the heat, but it was a harmonium, a keyboard with pedals. If you pedalled hard, it produced a sound like the death throttle of a dying goat, though it did so at a wide and somewhat arbitrary series of intervals.

This instrument was kept in the camp chapel, where I played the hymns on Sundays, being the nearest thing to a musician on the base. When the MP found this out, he made a bargain with me. He would buff the floor for me, if I would play Handel's *Largo* on the harmonium. So I did. We would go the chapel when it was empty, I would squeak and pedal away at Handel's *Largo*, and he would weep softly on one of the chapel chairs, his huge shoulders heaving in time to the music. Then we would go back to the police hut, and he would buff the floor while I read a comic book. It was all very satisfactory.

Bahrain was supposed to be a really tough posting, but it had its compensations. There was a swimming pool that I visited every day, and BOAC (it turned into British Airways, I think) flights to Australia refuelled at Bahrain. So there was a BOAC restaurant virtually on the camp, where we could find things that were, for a change, edible. Virtually all of my pay went on that. Then there were my fellow Oiks (that is what we were called by everyone else). I have never before or since met such a wide variety of people, all stuck together in the middle of a sweltering hot house. There were public schoolboys waiting to go to university. There were Glaswegians whom nobody else could understand. There were boys who had been thrown out of school. There were boys who had barely escaped from prison, only to find that they were really still in prison. And there were even a few older men who had been in the RAF for some time, but had been demoted for some unmentionable reason, and were serving out their time with a sort of Stoical depression—but at least they had free food and clothing.

What they all had in common was that nobody wanted to be there. All I can say is that I saw and heard things that had never been seen or heard of in a Northern grammar school. I found it all very eye-opening, and I even made some very good friends. What I never quite understood was how we were all supposed to be contributing to the defence of the realm. I suppose that was the idea, but with all my training, the only thing I could think of was that if an emergency arose I could refuse to carry the enemies' bags, or perhaps I could put their files in the wrong order. Maybe I could send their letters to the wrong place. Perhaps there were things I could do, but on the whole it seemed to me that I was just being a drain on the country's resources. It is not surprising that I was, as it turned out, almost the last person ever to be called up to do National Service. After me, they gave up.

DUPLICATING IN ADEN

People were not allowed to stay in Bahrain for more than a year, because it was so hot and clammy, so I looked forward to being sent somewhere more obviously attractive. As I might have predicted, instead I was sent to Aden, in the Yemen, to complete my service to the nation. Aden was admittedly an improvement. The billets were smaller—only fifteen men in a room. They were on a hill, which meant they got some sea breezes from time to time. And there was a nearby port which, though it was home to terrorists and revolutionaries, at least had some shops in it.

We were not allowed to wear uniforms in the town. This was meant to be so the inhabitants would not realise that these pasty-faced white men in European dress were Brits from the nearby military base. I am not sure that this clever ruse worked, since there were no other pasty-faced white men around. But on my passport, under 'occupation,' it said 'government official,' not 'low-ranking military lick-spittle of the British occupying power.' I was rather proud of that, thinking it gave me some sort of status, and not realising that everyone else knew it meant 'clerk.'

There were real wars in Aden, real bombs and explosions. But, now having been promoted from 'aircraftsman, second-class' to 'senior aircraftsman' (SAC) because of my efficiency in filing, I had a little office of my own where I carried on duplicating (and usually smudging—not my fault, they were very old hand-operated duplicating machines) orders from HQ Aden Command.

This led to another of the mistakes that have filled my life. Much later on I was listed in some sort of American 'Who's Who.' Not knowing what an SAC was, they wrote that I was a member of Strategic Air Command, in Omaha, Nebraska—they were, I think, the people who dropped the atom bomb. How a young Englishman got into that outfit I cannot guess, but it did lead to some interesting encounters with members of the Campaign for Nuclear Disarmament.

A kindly officer gave me a reference when I left the Air Force, which read, "In command of printing facilities at Air Force headquarters, Aden." That referred to me and my Xerox duplicating machine, but to anyone who did not know that, it could have seemed quite impressive, though I never had to use that reference.

A DESERT REVELATION

The other strange thing that happened to me in Aden arose from the fact that I played the harmonium in the chapel, as I had done in Bahrain. My version of Rosicrucian Methodism had wavered a bit when I decided that some of the Rosicrucians were decidedly weird, and none of the Methodists seemed to agree among themselves, and were always splitting off into smaller and smaller new churches. They were all exceedingly nice people, but they just could not stop, if they were theosophists, having weirder and weirder ideas and, if they were Methodists, continually arguing about points so obscure that there was no possible way of deciding who was right.

What kept me going was that I still loved music, and the thought that, after all, I was a bit weird myself, and I really enjoyed arguments (this was to influence my future career considerably). So, I happily went on playing the harmonium. Then, for the first time in my life, I came across some very conservative Pentecostal Christians. The RAF chapel I went to was a collection of every Christian denomination that was not Anglican or Catholic. Anglicans had to dress up and go on church parades, and at that time I had never even been in a Catholic church. So, our chapel was the obvious place for people like me to go to. I was astonished at some of my fellow Protestants. They jumped about, waved their arms in the air, and made strange noises, claiming that they really loved Jesus and, more to the point, that Jesus really loved them (more than anybody else, it seemed). I was quite impressed. They were so fervent and enthusiastic. Since I could not always escape when they invaded the chapel, I joined them. And the most peculiar thing happened. I actually had a vivid experience of Jesus, not visual, but real nonetheless.

I was never quite as enthusiastic as they were, and I was never persuaded by their very literal interpretations of the Bible. But the experience of a spiritual power working (and felt) within me, was undeniable. It gave me a renewed sense of direction, and a feeling that life was good and meaningful, even in Aden, doing things that seemed completely pointless.

I have to say that I have never lost that sense. It was a sort of invasion of goodness and love into my humdrum life. I think of it as a sense of what Matthew Arnold called "a power making for righteousness." St. Paul spoke of "Christ in you, the hope of glory," and that seemed a pretty good description to me of a transformative experience of a spiritual power founded on faith (encounter with a reality of transcendent goodness), empowered by love (sharing in a spiritual power greater than my own), and evocative of hope (for the fuller realisation of that power in my life and in the world).

The odd thing was that I never connected this sense of an inner spiritual power with the doctrines that my new friends believed. They believed that the world was created in six days, and their only problems were things like how long a 'day' was, especially before the sun had been created (which might have provided a valuable clue). They were also very keen to know exactly when Christ would come again, and haul them up into the sky, leaving everyone else behind. I personally hoped that I would have time to get back to England and see my family again first.

Of course, not all of them thought like that, and I realised that whatever people think about a moral or religious question, other people will disagree. True, people need some sort of affirmation, and they will get into small groups which all agree on some topics. But they must really know that there are lots of other groups that agree on different things, so it is most unlikely that only their group is right. Furthermore, if they talk long enough among themselves, they will inevitably find something to disagree about. In the end, the only person you will completely agree with is yourself. Even then, there is always the danger that you will change your mind—in my case, almost every day.

The best course might seem to be to become agnostic. But that is impossible. If you meet someone you really like, and they say, "Do you love me?," it is unhelpful to say, "I am agnostic." There are some things you just have to have an opinion about, at least in practice. One of them is religion. You either pray or you don't.

I did not realise at the time, but I was turning into a philosopher, people who have problems very few other people have even thought of, and who know so many possible solutions that they cannot remember which one they accept.

For the moment I put all these thoughts aside and concentrated on my harmonium. If you have ever tried playing Rachmaninov's Second Piano Concerto on a harmonium, you will know how difficult it is. You have to pedal so hard that you will be exhausted before you get to the second movement.

CARDIFF, 1958–1962

I ATTEMPT TO BECOME A MUSICIAN

In Aden, I met another National Serviceman who told me he was going to Cardiff University, which had a very good music department. So, I applied to them, explaining that it would be difficult for me to go for interview, since I was in Aden, and only had a harmonium, but that at least I had got music at scholarship level while at school.

They accepted me, and as soon as I was ejected from Her Majesty's Service, I began to study for a Bachelor of Music degree at what was then the University College of South Wales and Monmouthshire, part of the University of Wales. My choice turned out to be another mistake.

The university was not a mistake. It was a wonderful place in a wonderful city. My choice of studying for a BMus was the mistake. Two years of playing the harmonium had not prepared me for learning how to compose music in the styles of Palestrina and Haydn, and how to distinguish an augmented fourth from a diminished fifth. The course concentrated on composition, and my compositions were so lamentable that they managed to break all the rules of harmony while failing to produce a single memorable tune.

Worst of all, I found that I just could not come to terms with contemporary music. It was very different from Handel's *Largo*, which could move military policemen to tears. At that time the composer Schonberg had invented something called 'twelve-tone' music. The idea was that you took all the twelve semitone notes in an octave and then wrote them down in an order you selected, to make up a piece, using various instruments, rhythms, and chords. There was no tune, and no key signature. I duly wrote a piece of twelve-tone music and handed it in. I could see that my tutor looked rather taken aback. He sat for a few moments, and then said, "Do you like this?" "Yes," I replied. The final straw was when he accepted it and even gave it decent mark.

That was when I decided that a career in music was not for me. I did love music, but it soon became apparent that I was stuck into a sort of late-Romantic time warp. I particularly liked Wagner, Richard Strauss, and Mahler—the composers of admittedly grandiose music with huge orchestras and heavy emotional power. But such things had become virtually obsolete. Already in their works a sort of disintegration had begun, as they often parodied their own compositions, and the dissonances in their music grew more pronounced. In much of the more modern music, tunes and harmonies have been replace by 'sound worlds,' and there are rarely melodies that could easily be sung, or harmonies that have the power to evoke deep emotions. I could think of no way of writing in the modern style that was anywhere near bearable, let alone beautiful. Some people have the imagination and skill to do it, but it became clear to me that I could not.

At the same time, I never recovered the pianistic techniques that I used to have before my struggles with RAF harmoniums destroyed them. Without practicing for six hours a day for a couple of years, I would never make the grade as a concert pianist. Looking ahead to the rest of my life, I saw years of being a very good, but not excellent, pianist, being a really bad composer, and probably teaching music to classes of kids who, if they were as bad as I had been, were interested only in humiliating their indifferent teachers.

I had to get out. I had a feeling that I was good at something, but I did not know what it was. Worst of all, I found that the critical study of music was actually destroying my love of music. I was a born devotee of music, but a very bad creator of it. I did write some pieces, and even wrote what was probably the worst musical in history, though no one will ever know for sure, since I burned them all long ago. All my fault, I know, but there it was. Despite all the successes of my subsequent career, I have always really regarded myself as a failed musician. This, though rather sad, has been quite good for me, as it has always prevented me from thinking that I really was, as my mother thought, God's gift to the world.

The trouble was that I was in receipt of a government grant (called a state studentship) because of my good examination results in my final year at school, which paid all my fees and also gave me enough to live on (those were the days). I have to say that I would never have gone to university if I had to do what more recent students have to do, pay their own fees. But I was in the wrong course, even in the wrong faculty (music, not arts), and I could not get out of it.

ON THE BUSES

Then I discovered a loophole. I found out that I could transfer to the Faculty of Arts from the Faculty of Music, from a BMus to a BA. But I would have to finish one year of my course, start again from scratch in the new faculty, and pay my own fees for the first year. That is what I did. I was determined not to ask my father for money, so I got a job as a bus conductor (there were such things in those days) on Western Welsh buses, and worked all the overtime I could get, and lived on bread and jam (I believe this becomes 'jelly' if you cross the Atlantic)—with potato crisps (which turn into 'chips' in the States) for a treat on Saturdays—all one summer vacation; in fact, for all the summer vacations of my new three-year BA course. That paid my fees and expenses for a year.

During that time I met the attractive young women who was to become my wife, and I managed to persuade her to supply me with some proper food from time to time—a scheme that still continues to this day, with even greater effectiveness. (My daughter tells me that this is a sexist remark, but I have to say that it is just true that my wife's cooking is infinitely superior to mine, and that I am extremely grateful to receive it. If this is sexist, I can only ask what else one can expect of my virtually obsolete generation.)

Working on the buses in South Wales had its problems. The main one was that I could never understand where people wanted to go. The buses went up and down the Welsh Valleys, and there were lots of places with names like Llwnypia and Penrhiwceiber, which I could neither spell nor pronounce. If a passenger asked for a ticket to Llwnypia, I would not have the slightest idea where this was, and I used to issue tickets at random. This went down quite well with the passengers, who were on the whole paying much less than they were used to. Part of my job was to ring the bell, to tell the driver to stop where someone wanted to get off. Naturally, I did not know where this was, so I had to wait until people started shuffling in their seats to guess when they had arrived at their destination. I did get a few complaints about this, but generally they did not mind walking a little bit further, considering the cheap fare they had usually paid.

FIRST CONTACT WITH PHILOSOPHY

Back in the Faculty of Arts, I had to take three subjects in my first year. I chose industrial relations, thinking that because of my industrial experiences on the buses, I knew quite a lot about that already, English, and a subject new to me, philosophy. At last, I found the subject I had all my life been looking for. No matter how many ridiculous questions I had asked myself, philosophy had already asked them. Not only that, it had given even more ridiculous answers to them. Why is there something rather than nothing? was a good example. There is no possible answer to that question, but that did not stop philosophers answering it. One answer is that if anything is actual, it must always have been possible. Even if there was nothing, it must still have been possible. But things that are possible can only exist in something actual. Therefore, there must be an actual thing in which all possibilities, including the possibility of itself, exist. This is probably God, though for all we know it might have been almost anything.

If this argument intrigues you, you are a born philosopher. If it sounds like a piece of nonsense, you are more like a normal person. I am definitely not a normal person, because that argument really appealed to me as soon as I heard it. Neither was Plato, for that is whom I got it from. In fact, Plato thought that all possibilities (he called them essential natures, or 'Forms') were *more real* than actual things, which were just the half-real shadows of eternal possibilities. You can hardly get less normal than that. As those who do not like Plato very much say, they would prefer an actual pint of beer to a purely possible pint, even if the possible pint is more real, according to Plato.

I think the world divides into those who think this is a profound question, and those who think it is nonsense (although there is a third, pretty large, division of those who never think about it at all). It turned out that I did pretty well in philosophy. My random thoughts about Plato, possibilities, and actualities were no longer regarded as futile mental aberrations, but gained high marks in essays. After a year I was accepted into the Honours School of Philosophy.

It is interesting to look back on what we studied. We read Plato and Aristotle in detail, but then nothing philosophical happened until

Descartes, who apparently invented modern philosophy. We did not touch any Muslim or Indian thinkers, and regarded Thomas Aquinas as a sort of second-rate imitator of Aristotle—Thomas the tinker, one Oxford philosopher called him. This was obviously not a Catholic education, for Catholics tend to think that Aquinas is perhaps the most important philosopher ever.

Our main grounding was in the British empiricists, Locke, Berkeley, and Hume, and in the Enlightenment 'rationalists'—Leibniz and Kant in particular—and then we leapt straight into what was then contemporary 'Oxford' or ordinary-language philosophy. The German and English idealists from Hegel onwards went unnoticed, and modern continental thought was largely ignored. I remember that later, when the French philosopher Derrida was given an honorary doctorate at Cambridge, an eminent British philosopher remarked that Derrida would not even have passed the 'eleven-plus' primary school examination. That was how wide the gulf was.

Formal logic was a major part of the course, and we learned how to translate ordinary English words into pseudo-mathematical symbols, and derive wildly improbable conclusions from absurdly restricted and precise premises. This was basically a form of Boolean algebra, and it struck me at the time that this sort of thing, which became the basis for computer programming, usually managed to omit all the interesting nuances of the English language, eliminate anything like irony or ambiguity, and leave one with a very impoverished and inhuman version of reasonable discourse.

In a word, our philosophical training was very scholarly, clear, and precise within its limits, but it was also extremely limited in its range and understanding of other philosophical traditions. The irony was that the British empiricists were themselves idealists. An idealist, in philosophy, is not somebody who has all sorts of unrealistic expectations of a happy future. It is somebody who thinks that the whole material world is a product or expression of a reality that is in some way mind-like. The British empiricists were idealists, in the broad sense that they thought the whole basis of knowledge was what they called 'ideas,' which were mental entities. Some of them even held that the whole physical world was somehow constructed out of these ideas—and that is quite a strong form of idealism, which claims that the physical world itself is a derivative construction of minds, so that mind is prior to matter.

It is not, I think, generally realised that the major British philosophical tradition is idealist. But that is because the word 'idealism' came to be equated with the very obscure works of people like Hegel, who were just not British. The British reaction was to say that good plain common sense is more reliable than any verbose and overblown theory about 'ultimate reality.' However, it should be remembered that Bishop Berkeley, one of the 'big three' British empiricists, thought that idealism just was common sense. This just goes to show that it is very difficult to say what is common sense and what is not.

In accordance with my training, I developed an interest in Immanuel Kant. He was a Prussian philosopher who is often thought to have destroyed all possible arguments for God. This is rather ironic, since his whole life was devoted to showing that it was necessary to believe in God, though he did say that nobody could ever prove that God existed. It was a matter of faith, or basic belief. Also, what he said was so complicated that hardly anybody understands what he meant. Even those who do understand it disagree about what it was.

His work was of course written in German, a language that has the interesting habit of putting its verbs at the end of sentences. Kant wrote in very long sentences, which could end up with such a long string of verbs that it was impossible to tell which verb connected with which piece of the preceding sentence. It actually did not seem to matter very much. He also invented a whole set of unintelligible terms, like 'transcendental logic,' 'the schematism of the pure concepts of understanding,' and 'the paralogisms of pure reason.' That was just the sort of thing that gave idealism a bad name in Britain. The person who lectured us on Kant was keenly aware of the oddity of these terms, and he used to quote sections of the philosopher's writings, and immediately burst into fits of giggles, which failed to give us a sense of the importance of Kant's work.

I suppose the most important thing about Kant is that he was an ideal- ist (naturally, he called his view 'transcendental or critical idealism,' just to make sure nobody quite understood what it was). Most classical philoso- phers are idealists, though they disagree about what the mind-like basis of physical reality is. Some, like Leibniz, think it is God. Some think it is just a world of mathematical formulae, or abstract information, and so not at all like a person, though it is certainly not material, and it sounds extremely boring to most people. Immanuel Kant thought that there was a deeper reality, but nobody knew what it was except him, and he was not telling.

Freddie Ayer, a famous atheist who later became one of my teachers at Oxford, was an idealist, though most people, including him, never re- alised it—in fact, in his early life he vehemently denied it. He was an idealist because he thought that physical things were just logical constructions out of actual or possible sense-contents, and though he insisted that sense-contents were neither mental nor physical, in the ordinary sense, they must certainly be counted as private experiences, which is just what idealists basically claim. Unlike Plato, Ayer thought there was no 'world of Forms' or of mathematical truths. There were just momentary experiences, which he called, rather misleadingly, 'sense-data.' But, he thought, there was most definitely not a God, to whom he had taken a strong dislike.

Idealism appealed to me, and so did Immanuel Kant. With my mixed theosophical/Methodist/Anglican/evangelical background, it made sense to me to say that philosophers are definitely talking about something, even though none of them can agree what it is. Yet whatever that something is, it is not the ordinary physical world that most people think they live in.

What is the meaning of life? (1959)

THINKING OF A JOB

Not all of my College life was lived on this refined and rather abstract plane. I did live in the real world as well. Besides bus conducting, I helped to found the Cardiff University Social Services Organisation (which still exists, I think). This was an organisation of students who did voluntary social work. For instance, I spent a year gardening for an elderly disabled lady. Having dug up all her favourite flowers, I moved on to other things before she found out. I sat on the Student Council, wrote for the student newspaper, acted in and produced plays for the Dramatic Society, and, as I have mentioned, met my future wife.

One degree over (1962)

All these things mysteriously flowed together to make me think I should be ordained as a Christian minister. If I did that, I thought, I could think abstract thoughts during the week, inflict them on a helpless congregation on Sundays, and generally annoy people by interfering in their lives by trying to be helpful. I could also definitely get published, if only in the parish newsletter, which could not very well reject my attempts at literature, and I could certainly find a way of using my acting talents in church, however bad they were. I could even play the organ when nobody else was available. Overall, I could probably help more people face to face than in any other job I could think of. There was always politics, of course. But I did not fancy kissing quite so many babies as a path to political power.

I had joined the Anglican Society in my second year, and it was run by a delightful priest called Father Davies, who was a priest of the Church in Wales because he thought Roman Catholics were no longer traditional enough. He was, as they say, extremely 'high', not on cocaine, but on incense and holy water. I liked the incense and the ceremony, and the general air of mystery that surrounded those ceremonies. It seemed very suitable for relating to the unknown reality that, I assumed, only Kant and I knew about.

In due course, I went to the bishop of Llandaff to see about getting ordained. Then I made yet another mistake—this seems for some reason to be a continuing theme in my life. I mentioned to the bishop that I did not think that the 'Hail Mary' should be said aloud, as it was during Anglican services run by the Anglican chaplaincy. The evangelical bit of my background made me remember that many Anglicans were not very keen on the Virgin Mary (after all, Mark's Gospel says that at one stage she tried to stop Jesus preaching, or even, on some interpretations, thought that he was beside himself—see Mark 3:21 and 31), and they did not like to hail Mary very often, or even at all. The bishop, who was as 'high' as Father Davies, said, "Well, if you think like that you had better go to Wycliffe Hall." This was a theological college in Oxford, of a distinctly evangelical sort, in some ways not unlike the RAF chapel I had attended in Aden. My going there was a sort of penance imposed by the bishop.

I was not sure about this, but the college was near the centre of Oxford, and I rather liked the thought of living there. So, after I gained a first-class honours degree in philosophy, answering all my questions in the style of Kant, so that nobody could quite understand them (which turned out to be just what the examiners liked), I went to Oxford.

OXFORD, 1962–1964

A RAILWAY INTERLUDE

BEFORE I GOT THERE, I had something of a financial crisis. My state studentship had run out, and though the Church was kindly going to pay for my tuition at Oxford, I had nothing to live on during the summer. I needed to get a job quickly, and the only thing I could find was as a railway porter at Clapham Junction. I convinced them that, because of my RAF career, I was very good at carrying bags, and I said that I would love to use my expertise to help British Rail. They were rather concerned that I might be overqualified, with a degree in philosophy, but when I told them what philosophy was, they agreed that I was not really qualified for anything.

I enjoyed my time at Clapham Junction, with thirteen platforms and hundreds of trains. I ran up and down the platforms with a little cart, helping people with their luggage, and telling them which trains left from which platform—unfortunately I often got this wrong, but by the time they realised this they were already on the way to somewhere unexpected. I also delivered parcels to various flats in Clapham, as an assistant parcels operative. I assisted a much older and wiser man, who used to take a parcel and disappear into some of these flats for suspiciously long periods of time, leaving me in charge of the van. I was very good at sitting in the van, and my manager told me that if I carried on like this, I might soon get an office job. However, at the end of the summer I had to resign my rather promising career on the railways, and begin my studies at Oxford.

This was a two-year course in theology, which included learning how to baptise babies without drowning them, how to marry people without getting their names mixed up, and how to persuade people at funerals not to choose "All Things Bright and Beautiful" as their funeral hymn. There was also quite a lot of reading the Bible, praying, and confessing of sins, which required a good deal of judicious selection from the wide variety of possible sins—many more were possible than even I had realised—that were available.

A JOURNEY TO JERUSALEM

One of the things I did at Wycliffe Hall would be quite impossible today. Six of us obtained an old Morris Oxford car, and drove it from Oxford to Jerusalem, on a sort of automated pilgrimage to the Holy Land. It was an increasingly smelly journey, with six people crammed into a rather small car, I have to admit, but the smell was well worth it. We passed through what was then Yugoslavia, Turkey, Syria, and Jordan in sublime indifference to the political convolutions that were taking place. In Syria we were looked after by some very kind soldiers, who allowed us to sleep in their camp overnight. They were, we discovered, the secret police, though I was not sure whose side they were on. Nor did they know for sure whose side we were on. They did, however, guard us very well—we heard them marching up and down outside our tents all night—and sent us on our way, having decided that the car was so old that we could not possibly be spies.

The one annoying thing about the journey was that my companions refused to plan ahead about where we might sleep or obtain food and petrol. I thought it was only rational to make some sort of plan about these things, but they just said, "The Lord will provide." What was annoying was that the Lord did provide, though I privately thought that it was just good luck. Each night we found somewhere quite pleasant to erect our tents (even including in the secret police camp in Syria), and the one or two inevitable mechanical problems that occurred were always within hailing distance of helpful and curious inhabitants. Even when the car broke down just outside Samaria, we were welcomed into the home of a genuine good Samaritan, who was intrigued to find that we all slept together at nights (we took our wives or girlfriends with us), and brought all the neighbours round to observe our barbaric customs.

When we got to Jordan, we could not say that we were going to Israel, as the border guards did not admit that such a place existed. We had to say that we were just going to see the desert, and they warned us that though we were welcome to do that, we would not be able to come back. I think they really knew where we were going, but they were glad to get rid of us. We made the mistake of entering Jerusalem on the Sabbath, and were met with hails of stones from the Orthodox. But we succeeded in our plan to see the holy places of early Christendom, and then managed to catch a car ferry to Istanbul, thus avoiding the Jordanian customs officials who were waiting to impound us on our return.

We slept below decks, having run out of money, and the women with us, including my wife, had to give up their underwear to a group of very large Turkish ladies who took a liking to Western lingerie. We then proceeded back to Oxford as fast as the car would go, which was not really very fast, and felt that we were much better prepared to study Christian theology after we had experienced the places of its origin. The journey reinforced my belief that Jesus was definitely not an Anglo-Saxon with blue eyes and a pale face, as he seemed to be portrayed in many Western works of art. He was definitely dark-skinned and semitic, and belonged to a culture as different from that of Merrie England as it was possible to get. Perhaps he was so alien to people like me that we would have great difficulty in understanding him (especially since he spoke Aramaic, which nobody bothered to write down, so we do not know exactly what he said). What this would do to my theology was, at that stage, not entirely clear.

THEOLOGICAL TRAINING AND THE BIBLE

Some people think that the study of theology indoctrinates people with a set of dogmas that they just have to accept on authority and without question. In fact, the sort of theology I studied at Oxford did just about the opposite. It involved the study of lots of dogmas that were clearly wrong (those were the dogmas held by members of other churches, of course). But the study implied, though of course it did not state, that the dogmas held by our church were probably just as mistaken. After all, why should we be the only people who had the truth?

It revealed that most of the books of the Bible were not written by the people we thought had written them, and were filled with legends and exaggerations as well as with a few descriptions of things that may actually have happened—though it was difficult to tell which was which.

A good example is the stories of the birth of Jesus. If we have seen the nativity plays that schools used to put on at Christmas, we will know that there were three kings from the Orient who came to the stable where

Mary and Joseph and the baby were. The kings were so well known that they even had names. When we read the Bible, however, we find that we do not know how many 'Magi' visited Joseph and Mary; their names are never mentioned; they might have been Zoroastrian priests; they were almost certainly not kings; and they did not come to the stable with a bunch of shepherds. They visited Mary in a house, some time later.

What this tells us is how stories grow and get more detailed as time goes on. In cultures all over the world, there are stories of the miraculous births of great men. The traditional story of the birth of the Buddha, for example, is that as soon as he was born, he stood up, took seven steps, and said, "I alone am the world-honoured one." We do not hesitate to call this a legend, and there is no reason for modern Buddhists to believe it actually happened. Krishna is said to have balanced a mountain in his hand. Closer to our own time, Sai Baba produced magic dust out of thin air. Among the saints of Christendom, St. Uncumber (a lady) grew a beard overnight to put off the man who had been chosen to be her husband. Not surprisingly, he changed his mind.

We might expect that legends would grow up about Jesus. One of the stories about Jesus that did not get into the Gospels (though it got into the Qur'an) is that when he was a boy, he made some clay birds, and they proceeded to fly away. That does sound very like a legend to me.

There are other things said about Jesus that we find it hard to believe. One of his main activities was to exorcise demons, and they talked to him and grumbled as they were cast out. We might be suspicious of some modern-day psychiatrists, but casting out demons is not usually one of their skills. To be frank, we do not believe demons cause diseases at all.

The more I read the Bible carefully, the clearer it seemed to me that there was a lot of legend and exaggeration in its accounts. And there were bits in it which were hard to take. Did God really tell the Israelites to exterminate Canaanites who did not simply surrender their property? Did God really kill everyone who touched the sacred ark, even accidentally? Both these things are recorded in the Old Testament, as Christians call it.

There is a way of dealing with this, which is very obvious when you think of it. These legends and quasi-magical beliefs are stages in the development of the idea of God in Hebrew thought. That idea developed through the ages, from thought of one tribal deity among others to the later thought that there is one creator God who is perfectly good and cares for the welfare of all sentient beings. That is a much more morally satisfactory idea, though it does leave us with the problem of why God created such a lot of suffering in the world.

When I studied the Bible in depth, I came to think that, like most of the literature of its age, it was a mixture of fact and imaginative fiction. Its accounts of historical events—including the life of Jesus—were often not straightforward factual accounts. They were symbolically enhanced narratives. They used stories of often extraordinary physical events, which may well have had some basis in fact, but told in such a way as to point more clearly to spiritual states and processes. For example, a story of Jesus changing water into wine (John 2:1–11) could be used to depict the new spiritual life and power that he breathed into what might have seemed to be formal religious rituals. I did not mind about this, but it certainly undermined the view that the Bible was an inerrant source of all wisdom. Instead, it is a record of the developing and changing interactions of the Jewish people with what they regarded as spiritual reality. But when I said this to my tutors at the end of my theology course, their response was to suggest that it might be better if I did not get ordained as a priest after all.

Another factor was that in my second year at Wycliffe I had married the girl I had pursued in Cardiff since the History Faculty outing to Raglan Castle. My tutors forbade this, saying that getting married was a bad influence on candidates for the priesthood, and would stop me getting up in time for Morning Prayer. But I ignored them, and we married in Llandaff Cathedral, where I had practised playing the organ during my regrettably aborted music degree. My tutors were right about Morning Prayer, and I think they viewed me with some suspicion after that.

My marriage did cause some changes at Wycliffe Hall. I had to take some practical instruction from a local parish priest, and I took my new wife along. I engaged in theological discussion with the vicar, while my wife was taken into the vicarage kitchen by his wife, and taught how to make cucumber sandwiches and do other suitably feminine things. We were so incensed by this that we rebelled to such effect that such visits were deleted from the syllabus and never occurred again. Indeed, now there are many married students at Wycliffe, and I thought it very ironic that I have been asked to contribute to the building of new married quarters, when I myself had been forbidden to get married. As a matter of principle, I stipulated that no-one, male or female, should ever again be taught to make cucumber sandwiches.

Fortunately, like many members of the theological college at that time, I had also taken a research degree at the University of Oxford, matriculating through Linacre College, of which I turned out to be a founding graduate member. It was possible to do a two-year course for a Bachelor of Letters (now an obsolete degree, rather like me) in philosophy, at the same time as preparing for ordination. The person who most influenced me then was Ian Ramsey, who was professor of the Christian religion, and who later became bishop of Durham. His book, *Religious Language* (1957), was an interesting blend of British empiricism and a rather liberal Christian faith. Under his influence, I wrote a thesis on the use of Heidegger by Rudolf Bultmann, the former being a German philosopher whose most famous philosophical remark, at least among sceptical British philosophers, was that "the Nothing noths" (*das Nichts nichtet*, which sounds better in German, though it still breaks all known grammatical rules), and was regarded by them as a prime example of nonsense. Bultmann was a German theologian who believed even less than I did. The thesis was successful, but this did not please my Wycliffe tutors very much, as they regarded most German theology as completely unsound. Nevertheless, on the strength of it, since I was not going to be ordained, I did the next best thing, and applied for jobs teaching philosophy in British universities.

GLASGOW, 1964–1969

PHILOSOPHY AND IDEALISM

AT THAT TIME (THE early 1960s) quite a few new universities were being built, so there were academic jobs to be had. Some universities quite liked the idea of having someone from Oxford who could teach philosophy. Today it is almost impossible to get a university lectureship in philosophy, largely because it does not train anyone to do anything in particular (as subjects like law, medicine, or chemistry are supposed to do). But in those days, having a general education in the history of ideas and a training in logic and critical thinking was considered a good foundation for life.

In Scotland, especially, philosophy was a well-established discipline. There were even two departments of philosophy in the ancient Scottish universities, one of logic and metaphysics and one of moral philosophy. I went for interview at Glasgow University (not exactly new—founded in 1451, the fourth oldest university in the English-speaking world) with an Oxford friend of mine. We were both applying for the same job, a lectureship in the Logic Department, leaving our wives back in Oxford wondering who would get the job. We wished each other good luck, with a small amount of mental reservation, as we both really wanted the job. In the event, the university offered us both lectureships (those were indeed the days!), which was a very pleasant surprise, and meant that mutual celebrations could be unconfined.

Glasgow University

When I started teaching philosophy, I had to consider what I had gleaned from my tuition at Cardiff and at Oxford. I had virtually been told that I was not a real Christian, but I was, I suspected, a real idealist. That was alright, because you can easily be an idealist without believing in God. David Hume, easily the most famous dead Scottish philosopher, had done so. And nobody in Scotland can teach philosophy without mentioning David Hume.

Hume had been an idealist (technically, a phenomenalist), in the sense I have outlined, thinking that all knowledge is, or should be, confined to ideas and what can be reliably inferred from them. But Hume was not very well disposed towards religion or God, so his philosophy was more like Buddhism (though he did not know that). Humans are just successions of perceptions, thoughts, and feelings, which are like long chains of transient mental events. There is nobody who 'has' these events, no self or soul or subsistent mind. There is certainly no God who somehow holds them all together. There are just chains of mental events, and the whole physical world is a logical construction out of these events.

I was not wholly convinced by this. Who does the constructing, I wondered, and how does it happen that so many different chains of mental events all seem to agree with each other when people (who do not really exist) all 'see the same things' (which do not really exist either)? The Oxford philosopher Freddie Ayer, whom I mentioned earlier, seemed to be a re-incarnation of David Hume, though he called Hume's ideas 'sense-contents.' I attended his lectures, even though, according to him, I probably did not really exist, since I was only a logical construction out of his sense-contents, and he himself did not exist either, since he was in turn just a logical construction out of my sense-contents. This did not seem a very satisfactory sort of existence to me.

Ayer claimed that he was dispensing with metaphysics (theories about the nature of reality). That was very odd, since it seemed to me that he was proposing a rather amazing metaphysics himself—namely, that the nature of reality was that it was really chains of sense-contents. Most other philosophers in Oxford did not believe what Ayer said. Two of them, Gilbert Ryle and Geoffrey Warnock, who taught me personally, insisted that there were no sense-data. They had just been invented by Ayer, and did not really exist. There were only people and things and three-dimensional objects in space, just as ordinary people thought. Of course, being Oxford dons, they did not really know what ordinary people thought, because they had never met any.

PHILOSOPHERS DISAGREEING

Gilbert Ryle was my moral tutor. When we met, he said, "I do not know what a moral tutor is, and I hope I never have to find out." I have to say that he never did. He was famous for saying that the mind is not a ghost in a machine—as if there is a little man inside my head thinking away and making decisions. He actually thought that there was nothing inside my head at all (which I thought was not very complimentary!)—that is, no separate centre of consciousness, only loosely connected to my brain.

When I told him that I had conscious dreams that did not connect with any of my behaviour, he said that was false. I had, he said, just woken up with the belief that I had dreamed, but I had never had any dreams at all. I could not see how to refute this, since I could never get back into my dreams to check if it was true. It turned out that Ryle did not ever dream. But I regarded that as a form of disability, and not a sound basis for philosophy. It was probably why he did not think there were any sense-data, which were private mental events, rather like dreams.

What Ryle was not was a materialist. There were not, in Oxford at that time, any materialists—people who thought that the real nature of reality was that it was made up of tiny material bits of stuff like electrons and quarks, and everything was made of very complicated arrangements of them. That, they thought, was so absurd it was not worth thinking about.

Little did they know that materialism was about to become the dominant philosophical view. How, after all, could arrangements of quarks, however complicated they were, start thinking about whether or not they were the only things that existed?

So there you are. My philosophical education left me with three completely different views of what really existed—either there was nothing but sense-data, (phenomenalism), or there was nothing but quarks and other sub-atomic wave-particles (materialism), or there was nothing but the world of three-dimensional solid objects, just as it appeared to ordinary common sense (ordinary-language philosophy). Still, they all managed to agree that whatever they thought, they were not doing metaphysics, which was a thoroughly bad thing, and had only been done by dead philosophers. I thought that they were all doing metaphysics but would not admit it. What was I supposed to believe, and teach?

I have found that many people think that philosophy is a profound and difficult subject, and that philosophy professors are wise and tolerant people who think critically and carefully before they speak and are free of dogmatic prejudices. I have not, on the whole, found this to be true. Many British philosophers have a deep contempt for European mainland philosophers like Heidegger, who say ridiculous things like "Nothing noths," and write, the English say, mostly gibberish. They also often have a contempt for many of their colleagues, whether that is because those colleagues believe in sense-data or because they don't. They speak as if their views are obviously true and that all sensible people believe them, even though they are perfectly well-aware that in the lecture-room next door some other philosopher is disagreeing violently with them.

As a result, the one thing I am sure of is that people disagree fundamentally about almost everything. Once you see that, you realise that there is no certainty to be had in human life, and that you just have to do the best you can to live with the uncertainties that at least seem to do the least harm and the most good to other people, and hope that you have not got everything totally wrong.

THE TOSS OF A COIN

With these thoughts in mind, I was happily prepared to pass on my confusions and uncertainties to lecture-rooms full of unsuspecting undergraduates. The lecture-rooms in Glasgow were full, simply because philosophy (or psychology) was a compulsory subject for all first-year humanities students. The rooms were also steeply raked, with tiers of benches ranged in a semi-circle in front of the lecturer. During lectures, the men who sat in the highest row at the back (they were always men) used to roll ping-pong balls very slowly down the steps, just to make their opinion of compulsory philosophy lectures quite clear.

In revenge, they were all set a standard reasoning test at the beginning of the year. After doing a year of formal logic, they were given another standard reasoning test. The result was always that they were less reasonable after a year of logic than they had been at the beginning. There is a lesson there somewhere for the designers of programmes for computers. Computers may be logical, but they are not reasonable.

Glasgow was a great place and a great university. My wife and I had two Scottish children while we were there—that was one of the few things in my life that was not either an accident or a mistake. She taught in the Gorbals (now demolished), then a byword for crime and poverty in Glasgow. She was given a leather strap to hit the girls in her class with, but never had the heart to use it. She once tried to send a girl to the headmaster instead, and the girl said, "Do your own dirty work." She never did use the belt, but she eventually got on famously with the girls, and the experience taught us both a lot about the kindness and charm of what can look like the roughest of humans.

After two years at Glasgow, it was decided that, for staffing reasons (there had to be a roughly equal number of lecturers in each philosophy department—oh happy days!), my colleague and myself would have to move to the Department of Moral Philosophy. Both of us were quite happy where we were, and we decided to toss a coin. I lost, and so I moved. By pure chance, the whole trajectory of my academic life changed, and I suddenly became a moral philosopher. It turned out that moral philosophy was a very contentious subject. So contentious that the cardinal archbishop of Glasgow forbade Catholics to attend lectures in moral philosophy at Glasgow University. It seemed that in his opinion we were teaching immoral philosophy. Since philosophy was a compulsory subject in the first year, that was quite difficult for students. At least one of my Catholic students went to confession after every lecture. I was already having an impact on the world, but not in a way I had imagined.

It also happened that the professor of moral philosophy, William Maclagan, had written a book about the relation of morality and religion, in which he held that they were independent of each other, and that morality should always take precedence. I became interested in that topic, and it became my first publishable book (I had already written some unpublishable ones). It was called *Ethics and Christianity* (1970). It was not a defence of Christian ethics, as at that time I would not have called myself a Christian, after my tutors at Wycliffe had told me that I was not one. But it was an account of what, if anything, was distinctive about a religious, and specifically a Christian, morality. (I know that some philosophers make a great show of distinguishing ethics from morality, but as far as I am concerned, they are the same thing, except that one word derives from Greek and the other from Latin.) My argument was certainly not that Christians are more moral than other people. I had met enough Christians to know that was not true. Anyway, Christians were always saying that they were miserable sinners, so *they* knew it was not true as well. In fact, the Christian problem was that they knew what they had to do, but they could not do it. This struck me as too paradoxical to be believed. But something about it kept nagging away at me, and it was clear that Christianity was not finished with me yet.

ST. ANDREWS, 1969–1971

IMMANUEL KANT AT THE SEASIDE

APART FROM ALL THAT, I had always had a secret longing to live in a little town by the sea if I ever got the chance. That chance came when a lectureship in moral philosophy was advertised at St. Andrews University. Now that I was a moral philosopher, I applied, got the job, and spent two very happy years there, during which nothing much happened. And that was the trouble. I would recommend St. Andrews to anyone, but for me, it was not the paradise I had hoped for. I had imagined sunny beaches and blue sea, and long lazy days walking in the gently washing waves. There was sea, but it was too cold to swim in. There was sun, but when the sun shone warmly the sea mist (the Haar) came in and covered everything in a damp cloud. There were refreshing sea breezes, but they were *so* refreshing that when I played tennis I had to serve into the tennis court next to mine, because that was where the gales blew the tennis balls. In fact, it was said that when the wind stopped, people began falling over, as there was nothing to hold them up. There was also a marked absence of palm trees and snorkelling opportunities. As for operas and ballets, they required a long and tiring journey to Edinburgh or Dundee—there were no motorways then. The final straw was that it was even further from Wales than Glasgow had been, and my wife suffered from the Welsh affliction of *hiraeth*, a form of homesickness.

Nevertheless, St. Andrews had a very good library, and while I was there I wrote a book on the development of Kant's ethics. Kant had suffered from the same affliction that I had, a belief that if I ought to do something I must be able to do it—"ought implies can," is a statement widely attributed to him, though he never actually said it. It sounds very odd to say "Ought implies can't," and yet, contrary to popular belief, it was nearer to what Kant thought. Perhaps because of his Christian heritage, he held that there are absolute obligations, but we are unable to fulfil them. Life becomes a permanent struggle to do the impossible. No wonder so many Christians are depressed. I argued that Kant never solved this problem, largely because he was very much opposed to 'fanatical' experiences of God that might have made things feel better. Yet it is true that he was not the extremely rationalist and unfeeling moralist that he is widely thought to have been. He had feelings, but nobody ever knew what they were.

Kant propounded so many paradoxical and complicated thoughts that this made him a particularly interesting philosopher. He did not leave a coherent and clear systematic view of anything. He was a key figure of the rationalist Enlightenment, and yet he was deeply sceptical of the pretensions of reason (after all, his major works were called 'Critiques,' not defences, of pure reason) and he had a profound faith in something that he professed to know nothing about, and that nobody has ever been able to pin down. Or so I argued, and somebody thought enough of it to offer me a job teaching and researching in the philosophy of religion at King's College, London. This combined two of my chief interests perfectly. In this job, I could explore and examine some of the main ideas of religion (not just Christianity, but Buddhism and Tantra too, when I got bored). I could not resist the offer, and with a slight pang of sadness, I left St. Andrews for London.

KING'S COLLEGE, LONDON, 1971–1976

EXPERIMENTS IN FAITH

WHEN I LEFT WYCLIFFE Hall, I had given up religious practice. If, in the Air Force, I had been what evangelical Christians call 'born again,' after my time at theological college I had more or less 'died again.' I suppose I became a spiritual zombie, one of the walking dead. After all, I had been told that I did not believe enough strange and improbable things to be a Christian. So I decided to believe what most philosophers in Britain now seem to believe. That is, nothing. I became an atheist, though admittedly not an absolutely contented one.

When I went to London, I realised that claiming to be an atheist was too dogmatic for an agnostic. How could you be quite so sure? Freddie Ayer always said that you couldn't be an atheist because the word 'God' was meaningless, and it is silly to say that you do not believe in something when you do not even know what it is.

Actually, Ayer changed his mind about this, and came to think that 'God' was an explanatory hypothesis. The trouble was, he thought, that it did not really explain anything. Once you had said that objects fall to earth because of gravity, it does not help to add that, in addition, God made them so do. Gravity is a good enough explanation. God is just a useless addition, and no scientist would ever appeal to God to explain why things happen.

Anyway, I was now being paid to ask whether this was true. Was God a useless and obsolete way of explaining why things happen? We had rented a house in New Barnet, in North London, for a year while we looked for somewhere to live, and there was a church nearby which seemed like a good place to try to find out. I decided to start going to church again, more as an observer than anything else, and see if, when people went to church, they were trying to explain why things happened.

Before I begin, I should emphasise that the church I am about to speak about has changed a great deal since the time, a long time ago, when I was there. In fact, the change began when I was there, and I really think it was probably because a small group of people were praying for a renewal of the church's life. And though I was certainly not responsible for that renewal, maybe the fact I was attracted to it had a lot to do with that small group.

The church was in the middle of a large council estate. Very few people went to it, and they were all of very mature age, to say the least. The vicar was depressed and depressing, the building was aesthetically challenging, and the services were almost as depressing as the vicar. Yet, strangely enough, I felt attracted to it. It is very hard to explain why. But part of it was that I felt a sort of sympathy and affection for the members of the small congregation. It was like going to a meeting of lonely pensioners who were clinging together to find some hope and comfort at the end of their lives. This may sound pathetic, but it was something more than that. It was as though, despite all the setbacks and disappointments of human lives, there was a place where something of transcendent and enduring value could for a moment or two be found.

It could not be said that it was a matter of deep theological insights, or of vibrant and triumphant faith. It was more like a shared perception of the sadness of human existence, and the sense of something that would enable one to endure and not give up hope. This was clearest to me when I went along to the little Bible study group. The group managed to discuss what St. Paul called his "thorn in the flesh" (2 Corinthians 12:7) for over two months, during which each member discussed their own ailments, at length, and wondered whether that was what St. Paul had. It could have been embarrassing, but what it showed me was the pain of so many lives, and the struggle to be kind and considerate in an often-uncaring world. These people were not trying to explain the world or anything half so grand. They were striving to find dignity and meaning in a largely indifferent environment. They had a quality of humanity that, I have to confess, was rare in the academic world.

When they went to church, they said they were sorry for the thoughtless and unkind things they had done, they expressed gratitude if anything good had happened, and they promised to try to do better in the coming week. There was nothing about the first cause of the universe or the plausibility of phenomenalism. There was much about getting on with the neighbours and coping with illness and disappointment, about celebrating small things and about the joys of simple friendship. Admittedly, they asked God to heal people who were ill, but it did not seem they really expected anything much to happen as a result, and their requests were on the whole much less effective than taking a few aspirins.

It was clear that this sort of religion, anyway, is not any sort of explanatory hypothesis. It is more like having a personal relationship with somebody whom you might sometimes almost catch sight of, whom you are trying to love, but who might not actually be there at all.

Anyway, attending that unprepossessing church was another turning point in my life, and I found that finding real fellowship with people who were not at all academic, which I did for all my life from that time on, kept me rooted in human realities and friendships that made my approach to philosophy much more concerned with human experiences than might otherwise have been the case. Philosophy is concerned with ultimate problems of understanding and meaning, but it can become a highly technical pursuit. That is only right and proper. But philosophy should also be the search for practical wisdom in dealing with human anxieties and expectations, and thus needs to stay in touch such everyday realities. My renewed contacts with church life made this possible for me, and I have always valued that enormously.

Of course, membership of a church usually goes along with some sort of belief in God, however vague. Relationship to God can sometimes be put too simplistically by thinking of it as though it was a straightforward relation to a supernatural person. Something had to be done about that, from a philosophical point of view.

THE RETURN OF GOD

Ayer was sure that such a supernatural person did not exist. The irony is, however, that his form of logical positivism could easily suggest that there was such a person. After all, for Ayer all sense-data were private, and you could never have anyone else's sense-data. So Ayer had a major problem about the existence of the sense-experiences of other people, which were things you could not observe. He did have ways of trying to solve this problem, but it is generally agreed, and he told me in person that he even came to think himself, that they are not wholly satisfactory. It does seem that there are many sets of sense-data, some of them experienced by persons and animals very unlike you, that could never be experienced by you.

It is therefore reasonable to suppose that there are lots of sense-data that exist, which you never experience. They are presumably experienced by some other persons or person-like beings. It is quite a small step from there to thinking that the public and largely unobserved world of physical objects could be a total set of sense-contents (and thoughts) of a cosmic person, whom you can never observe, since that cosmic person would have no particular physical body the behaviour of which you could detect. This might very well be God. It may be that such a proposal is more plausible than the thought, proposed by Ayer in *Language, Truth and Logic* (1936), that the objective but unobserved physical world is no more than a set of possible perceptions by human beings, because, being only possible, they are only dubiously actual.

Ayer's view is in fact very like what the eighteenth-century philosopher Bishop Berkeley had said. Reality consists of 'ideas'; ideas are in minds; what we call physical reality is really the content of a huge cosmic mind. Therefore, a cosmic mind, God, exists. Ayer, of course, did not believe in minds as containers of ideas. Nevertheless, for him the physical world has to be more like collections of experienced events than it is like a collection of physical and unconscious objects.

This theory was so weird that I was tempted to believe it. (It was the quantum physicist Niels Bohr who said that some theories are just not weird enough to be true.) If it was true, then when I went to church, I too could talk to the personal being who had in his (or her) mind all the experienced events that I called the physical world. I would obviously know that this person was not very much like a human being. He (or she) did not have a beard, like Michelangelo's picture of God in the Sistine Chapel, and did not have testicles, like a man. God was more like an unembodied conscious, thinking, and feeling, reality that somehow held the whole universe in being. Without it there would be no universe at all.

THE SPIRITUAL DIMENSION

So it seemed to me that if Ayer was right, God was possible after all. Yet I still hesitated. Nobody else at Oxford had thought that Ayer was right, and the idea of talking to a person I could never actually see might seem a little childish. I thought again about my old supervisor, Gilbert Ryle, and his idea that philosophy was not really telling us mysterious things about the universe that scientists did not know. Instead, philosophy was about seeing how words were actually used, and how, when this was misunderstood, weird metaphysical theories—like the invention of sense-data, or belief in free will, or the idea that minds were little men hiding in the brain, 'ghosts in the machine'—came into being.

I was never completely convinced by this theory, as most Christians I know really did think there was a real person whom they addressed in prayer. The simple faith of the parishioners of New Barnet helped to show me that this was not some abstract theory about the nature of reality but a hint of another dimension of experience that promised to make some sort of sense of a perplexing and often troubled life. It was, to revert to the more theoretical, as I inevitably keep doing, a dimension of objective moral demand and moral hope, inherent in the universe itself.

By 'an objective moral demand' I mean that morality was not just, as Ayer thought, an expression of social or personal preferences. It was a demand that one should live in a loving way, and that demand was an objective reality, part of the furniture of the universe, not just a human invention. And this meant that there was a real moral hope, based on the ultimate nature of things, that people might one day become able to live in that way, instead of in the ambiguous and self-centred way that is so common. That was what some people in New Barnet thought. That was what Kant had thought, and what was good enough for New Barnet and for Kant was, I decided, good enough for me.

Maybe there was even some way in which the idea of a cosmic mind and of an objective moral demand could modify each other. There might be something that was not just an invisible and largely inactive superman (the caricature of a cosmic person), and not just an unconscious and impersonal moral law (the caricature of an objective moral demand), but a moral dimension to existence that was somehow personal in nature.

Once that idea was formed, it was easy to see my first love, music, as a disclosure of a something that was not just a subjective whim, but an apprehension of some objective source of transcendent beauty. And my second love, philosophy, could be seen, as its Greek etymology implies, as a love of wisdom, of a deep intelligibility and rationality underlying the way things are. Maybe these things could be integrated in the idea of a morally demanding, personal, intellectually elegant, and intelligible dimension to reality. Goodness, mind, beauty, and wisdom could be aspects of being that could be experienced in part, yet would always evoke a sense of something inexpressible, lying beyond language or description, and revelatory of the ultimate nature of the cosmos.

AN ACCIDENTAL ORDINATION

Anyway, those thoughts put God back on my agenda. With an amount of private interpretation, I could make some sense of church services again. Worse than that, some of my old evangelical experiences, which had taken such a battering in theological college, came flooding back. Not only that, even worse was to happen—and, as usual, it happened by accident. One day, I was given a message to take to the bishop of London. I arrived at his palace, and for some unaccountable reason, perhaps because I had been at Wycliffe Hall and was now teaching, among other people, theology students at King's College, he thought that I had come to talk about being ordained as a priest. He was probably aware that Wycliffe had told me I should not be ordained, because I was not even a proper Christian. But he was, after all, an Anglican bishop, of the sort that was not sure that Wycliffe Hall had a wholly secure grasp of Christian truth. In fact, he did not agree with Wycliffe Hall (as it was then) very much at all, and that made him even more determined that I ought to be ordained. So he began to discuss a date when he could ordain me (as a deacon in the first place) in King's College chapel.

At first, I was very surprised, but as I thought about it, it began to seem an attractive possibility. I had found, in New Barnet, that most people were not unduly bothered with abstract problems of theology. Faced with the difficulties and problems of everyday life, they sought some experience of a higher spiritual power that might alleviate feelings of guilt and despair, and give positive meaning to their lives. They sought what Paul Tillich called "the courage to be," a power of compassion and love greater than their own, in which they might share, however fitfully and imperfectly.

Maybe as a priest I could help in that search. I have to say that the academic life, though not exactly an ivory tower, was in many ways rather far removed from the daily lives and concerns of most people. Being a minister of a church would ground my rather abstract theories in practical contact with a much wider range of human lives and concerns. It might, as they say, keep my feet on the ground, and keep me in touch with the realities of anxiety, hope, disappointment, and desire, in what my father called 'the real world.'

There was another aspect, too. If I, as a philosopher, was ordained, it could help to show that commitment to a spiritual dimension of life was academically respectable and rationally defensible, and not just some sort of emotional prop for damaged souls. I did not foresee that later, when I became a theologian, and defended some interpretation of Christianity, people would say, "Well, he is a priest. He is paid to say that, poor thing." (Just as an aside, I never have been paid by the church, except for my training at theological college.) But that still lay in the future, so I accepted what seemed the natural thing to do (Christians call it 'the will of God'), and a year later I was ordained in King's College chapel.

I needed first to do a 'refresher term' at Westcott House, a theological college in Cambridge which was much less evangelical and more centrally Anglican than Wycliffe then was. I was interviewed by another friendly bishop, and we chatted amicably for a while about world affairs and the state of the church. As I opened the door to leave, he said, "By the way, how is your spiritual life?" "Oh, it is reasonably satisfactory," I replied, and that was apparently all that was needed. Anglicans are, after all, very reticent about what goes on inside people. As Queen Elizabeth I is reputed to have said, "I have no desire to make windows into men's souls." So for a term I played the organ (or was it a piano? I cannot remember) in Westcott chapel, became quite expert at bowls (it was summer), and learned that it was considered quite acceptable to be a priest and disagree with St. Paul, the unknown writers of the Gospels, and almost everybody else. What was really important was prayer and meditation, living in simplicity and fidelity to others, trying to care in practical ways for those we met, and finding beauty and goodness in the world around us. Why ask for anything more?

WORKING IN A PARISH

I continued to teach at King's, but when, after three months as a deacon, I became a priest, I also took an unpaid job as a curate at Hampstead Parish Church, in London. At this time, I wrote *The Divine Image* (1976), a small book that was supposed to be more popular than my big book on ethics and Christianity, and that took a much more positive view of Christian ethics. I sent a copy to my mother, explaining that it was a more popular book. "Oh no it isn't," she replied bluntly. My mother did not hesitate to be direct, and she was probably right. When I sent her copies of my books in future, I always put them in the dust cover of some detective story. I never knew if that helped. I also wrote *The Christian Way* (1976), a short account of a positive and creative Christian faith, dedicated to my new parishioners. Unfortunately, the publishers put a picture of Spaghetti Junction, in Birmingham, on the cover. This is one of the most complicated and frustrating of all motorway junctions in Britain and suggests that the Christian way is exceedingly hard to find, and probably to be avoided if at all possible!

I thought that in being a priest I was committing myself to a life of discipline and self-sacrifice. It was rather odd, therefore, that my very first duty was to officiate at a wedding, where I found myself obliged to consume large quantities of champagne and canapes. God moves in mysterious ways.

Another surprising parochial duty came along when a stranger knocked at the door of my house, where the previous curate had lived, and said, "Father, can you come at once to the hospital. A patient is asking for your urgently." "Are you sure it's *me* they want?" "Yes, Father." (It wasn't; it was the previous curate, I found out.) Anyway, I went to the local hospital, equipped with various prayers and hopefully uplifting verses, and found the patient. "Oh, thank God you've come, Father," he said. "These bloody nurses won't let me have a fag. Have you got one with you?" Those were my initiations into the priestly life. I must say that I enjoyed it tremendously, especially as, being only a curate, I did not have to take the blame for anything. Even when the vicar retired, and I found myself as priest in charge of a major London church for nearly a year, I could avoid all real responsibility by saying that I did not wish to annoy the next vicar by making any rash decisions of my own. This sort of masterly inactivity would have been approved of by Queen Elizabeth I, and it certainly worked for me.

WITTGENSTEIN CAUSES TROUBLE

It is incredible to realise how much things have changed since those days. At King's College, women lecturers, or even professors, were not allowed into the senior common room, however senior they were. They had to make their own coffee or buy some further down the Strand. In the Wig and Pen, a hostelry near the law courts, women were not allowed to order drinks, though they could at least sit in the bar. During my time at King's, in a burst of revolutionary fervour, the common room was opened to women. Unbelievably, the common-room staff, mostly ladies, resigned rather than serve coffee to women. No wonder that Rosalind Franklin, who was vital to the discovery of the double helix of DNA, had hated the place! Rosalind died before she could receive the Nobel prize for her work with crystallography, the radiation that killed her. (Her boss was one of the three men who did receive the Nobel prize in 1952, but nobody can ever remember his name. Everybody has heard of Crick and Watson, but who was the third man? He got so fed up at being unrecognised that he wrote a book called *The Third Man* [2003]. Unfortunately, nobody bought it, so he remains unknown. As it happens, though, I was friendly with him, and we often had lunch together. So I know that his name was . . . just a minute, while I try to remember . . . oh yes, it was . . . no, it's gone again, . . . sorry.)

Things on the philosophy side did not go quite so well as King's College. The professor who had appointed me, who shall remain nameless, turned out to be a control freak of the first order. He found out that, not only did I disagree with him on some philosophical points, but that I actually mentioned Wittgenstein with some approval in my lectures. I even wrote a book, *The Concept of God* (1974), which was very much influenced by Wittgenstein, and which tried to develop an idea of God that concentrated on the practical social contexts in which the word 'God' was seriously used, instead of asking what metaphysical entity the word stood for. This was one way of avoiding the sort of hard metaphysical problems in which Kant had got entangled and of locating the social and practical uses of God-language. It was seeing religion as a distinctive form of life with its own 'grammar,' and not primarily as a commitment to the existence of an abstract and invisible metaphysical entity. I later came to think that metaphysics was unavoidable, but Wittgenstein certainly focussed attention on the primarily moral and practical uses of the language of religion. However, my professor hated Wittgenstein, and ordered me to stop talking about the Cambridge philosopher, who, he thought, had besmirched the name of metaphysics (I suppose he had). I refused, and from then on, we were at daggers drawn. At faculty meetings he would turn around in his seat to see how I was voting, and if I voted the wrong way, he would not speak to me for a week. In many ways, this was a relief, but it made personal relations rather difficult.

CAMBRIDGE 1976–1983

THINGS GOT SO BAD that I decided I had to leave, with great reluctance. By chance, as usual, I came across an advertisement for the post of dean of Trinity Hall, Cambridge. This was a senior fellowship, whose duties involved counselling students, disciplining them for bad behaviour, and praying for them as minister in charge of the college chapel (there was also a college chaplain to help). Though these three activities, taken together, probably formed a self-contradictory triad, it sounded an interesting project. It also involved, in my case, being director of studies in philosophy and theology, which sounded ideal, so I applied and was interviewed. During the interview I managed to insult one of the interviewers by suggesting that his views were based on irrational prejudices, and I thought that was the end of that.

I heard nothing for months, and had forgotten all about it. But in early October I had a phone call: "Are you coming or not? Term has already started." The senior tutor had completely forgotten to tell me that I had got the job! It turned out that the person I had insulted was disliked by everyone else. Who could have guessed it?

When I got there, my counselling sessions were varied and fascinating. The one I remember best was with a brilliant mathematics undergraduate who was convinced that he did not exist. It was very difficult to talk to him, since he thought he was not there. But in the end I managed to convince him that we were both characters in a dream (which was what he suspected), that there was no way of distinguishing dreams from reality (that was where philosophy came in useful), and that the idea of a continuing self was probably an illusion anyway (that is where Freddie Ayer helped), so he might as well just accept that he was a chain of perceptions, thoughts, and feelings, keep calm and carry on. The last I heard he was happily writing games for computers, where nobody really existed, but they all had much more exciting lives than real people in the real world.

The disciplinary part of the job largely falls under the description of client privacy, so though many peculiar things happened, it does not seem right to talk about them. It is enough to say that it partly dealt with interpretations of the college rule that the same visitor could not share the room of a college student for more than one night. This was meant to prohibit long-term cohabitation, but it had the effect of promoting radical promiscuity, and later had to be amended.

Trinity Hall Library

CHAPEL MATTERS

As for the college chapel, it was probably the smallest chapel in Cambridge, and once the choir was in it, there was no room for anyone else. The choir was very large, possibly due to the fact that singers got a free meal after the service, and that the organist was extremely attractive. The fellows of the college on the whole did not attend, though they insisted that only the Authorised Version of the Bible should be used in services, just in case anyone understood what it was saying. They also insisted that the Thirty-Nine Articles of the Church of England must be adhered to, but since they had not read them, they were unable to check up on this. I put my faith in article 21, which says that general councils of the church have erred, even in things concerning God. I reckoned that if general councils of the whole church had erred, so with a high probability had some of the Thirty-Nine Articles of the much smaller Church of England. In that case, adhering to all the Thirty-Nine Articles would entail that some of them had probably erred. It follows that it was not possible to adhere to all the Thirty-Nine Articles, thank goodness. I was not a logician for nothing.

Like all deans and chaplains of Cambridge colleges, I had a little trouble with members of the tremendously popular Christian Union. This was probably the largest society in the university, and it took a strict Calvinist line on theology—something invented in the sixteenth century, though it claims to be just relating what the Bible says. Of course, many Christian churches say that, but it must raise some suspicions when you realise that they all differ from each other.

Having met members of this sect in the Air Force, I was wise to their ways, and quite sympathetic to their views, even though I now differed almost completely with them. So I took to visiting new undergraduates in their rooms when they first arrived, and if they seemed like potential members of the Christian Union, praying with them. This undermined their hostility, at least until they came to chapel and found out what I really thought.

I recall the college president of the Christian Union inviting me out to dinner. After the meal, he said casually, "Do you believe in substitutionary atonement?" This sounds like an exercise in mathematics, but due to having done National Service I knew what it meant. "Do you mean John Calvin's version?" I asked. But that was enough to condemn me. Naturally, as far as he was concerned, it was not 'Calvin's version,' propounded in the sixteenth century, but nothing more nor less than the unchanging biblical truth. So he said "It is probably better if we do not come to chapel." That was typical of Cambridge undergraduate religion. The evangelical churches were full, and the college chapels were empty. Except for ours, because we had such a large choir and such a small chapel.

Due to my vigorous praying activities, some members of the Christian Union did come to chapel, where they consistently corrected my theological views during the prayers. I would say, "O Lord, forgive us our sins." And one of them would stand up and say, "O Lord, we thank you that you have already forgiven our sins, before we even ask." I stood corrected.

One of the problems of Christianity, and perhaps of all religion, is that some of the faithful accept one particular set of beliefs—which originated as a theory devised by some particular person at some dateable point in history (as, for instance, the theory of penal substitutionary atonement did)—as if it was the absolute truth. Having the absolute truth, they are very keen to persuade everyone else about it, and since they have found eternal salvation, they are both terrifically enthusiastic and unduly pleased with themselves.

Meanwhile, the academic theologians and official college chaplains, who have all sorts of doubts and qualifications to make, are not very good at persuading others. They often only give people problems they had never thought of before, and they cannot guarantee eternal salvation even if you agree with them. Their product is just not marketable.

THE D SOCIETY

Philosophers in Cambridge when I was there were divided into different camps, members of which rarely spoke to each other. Of the two senior professors, one was a conservative Roman Catholic, and the other was a non-religious humanist. There was one devotee of Wittgenstein, and another who declared that the influence of Wittgenstein was dead. There was one who thought all decent thoughts should be put into rigorous logical form, and another who thought that formal logic was useless for solving (or dissolving) philosophical problems. The philosophers did not in general speak to the theologians, and the theologians did not speak to the philosophers. They each thought the others were too dogmatic to be worth talking to. I think I was the only person who lectured in both the philosophy and in the theology faculties, and as a result I quite often didn't speak to myself for weeks.

There was, however, a thing called the D Society, where selected university members could meet and discuss topics of interest. There are many such societies in Cambridge, and there is a widespread Cambridge fear that other societies that one has not been invited to join are more prestigious than one's own. Since one cannot get into the other societies, one never knows whether this is true.

It was at the D Society that I met the biologist Arthur Peacocke and the quantum physicist John Polkinghorne (both were also Anglican priests). I had always been interested in the natural sciences, and since I had taught symbolic logic, I had something of the requisite mathematical background. I found, however, that it was quite difficult for philosophers and mathematicians to communicate. Philosophers would look puzzled (that was their way of looking profound) and say, "Do imaginary numbers refer to anything?," and mathematicians would reply by writing longer and longer equations on the blackboard. This did not really help. Yet, with persistence some progress could be made. In particular, I found that mathematicians fell into two broad classes, those who thought that numbers really existed, and were the basis of everything, and those who thought that numbers were just invented by humans, and otherwise did not exist at all. With a sense of relief, I found that they were in that respect very like philosophers.

Numbers, it seemed, were a bit like God. Either (a) numbers existed, whether the physical universe existed or not; they could not fail to exist; and in some undefined way they produced the universe, or (b) numbers did not exist at all; they could not possibly exist, as there was nowhere for them to be; and they definitely had no role in the production of the universe, or in the production of anything. Pure mathematicians try to prove this by inventing mathematical systems that cannot possibly be used to produce anything. Unfortunately, their systems sometimes turn out to be very useful when constructing nuclear weapons and mobile phones. Nevertheless, there seems to be no way of deciding between these possibilities. Numbers really are a little bit like God.

There have been psychologists who have suggested that it is all a matter of potty-training. One lot of infant philosophers were anally retentive, and the other lot were anally over-productive, and that accounted for their later preferences either for a highly ordered and neat and tidy universe, or for a pretty random and accidental universe. I cannot now remember which was which, though I think it is the anally retentive who think the universe is highly organised and predictable. It was very difficult to gather evidence for this suggestion, as it was not something that philosophers usually talked about. I am not sure that there really was any evidence at all.

HOW SCIENTIFIC ADVANCES WERE MADE BY MEN OF RELIGIOUS SYMPATHIES

It was very clear, though, that modern science, especially molecular biology and quantum physics, was very relevant to philosophical and religious belief. Gone was the pre-evolutionary universe, when Eve was put together out of one of Adam's ribs, and dinosaurs were just too big to fit into Noah's ark (which is why there aren't any around). And gone was the earth-centred universe, where the stars were lights hung on the dome of the sky, and heavy objects were busy trying to get to the centre of the earth, because that was where they liked to be.

There have been many revolutions in physics since then, but though they have rendered the book of Genesis obsolete as a scientific account, they have not been free of religious influences. One of the first revolutions was the invention of the notion of laws of nature by Isaac Newton in 1687, a devout theist who believed that God, being very like Newton, would probably have devised the simplest set of laws that produced the richest set of effects, and would design the universe on an elegant set of universal laws. Newton turned out to be right. He also thought, despite having virtually invented the law of gravity, that objects could not affect one another at a distance. It was God who was responsible for long-distance gravitational effects. Newton kept this belief to himself for much of the time, and never discussed how God actually managed to keep so busy without ever being caught in the act.

Then Georges Le Maitre, a Catholic priest, discovered in 1925 that God had started the universe with a Big Bang. Mendel, a Catholic monk, discovered the laws of heredity by looking closely at some beans. Charles Darwin, who, he said, "had never been an atheist," but was (rightly) agnostic about many Christian claims, such as belief in an eternal hell, discovered evolution by natural selection. It was invented at the same time, around 1859, by Alfred Russel Wallace, and he was a spiritualist. In the nineteenth century, Faraday and Maxwell, both elders in Presbyterian churches, invented field theory and electro-magnetism. Einstein, an agnostic who nevertheless spoke favourably of the existence of a great cosmic intelligence, invented relativity and quantum mechanics, though they contradicted each other and he never really accepted the latter. However, in the early twentieth century Werner Heisenberg, a Lutheran, proved that quantum mechanics really worked. And Edwin Hubble, a Protestant who admittedly became less committed as time went on, discovered that there were galaxies beyond the Milky Way, so the universe was bigger than anyone had imagined.

This list—and it could be much longer—suggests two things to me. One is that many religious believers have been astoundingly creative scientists. What has driven much science is a belief that the universe is mathematically elegant and is a very rational enterprise altogether. It is not just one random accident after another—as though its laws might change overnight, and everyone might turn into a banana. It also seems that most of these creative scientists have not been completely 'orthodox,' not afraid of disagreeing with others, and putting out new ideas. That might be an important sign of a religious view that is truly compatible with good science.

The other thing this list suggests is that scientific understanding has changed dramatically, there is no reason to think that it is yet complete, and it is likely to change dramatically again.

HOW SCIENCE, PHILOSOPHY, AND RELIGION ARE ALWAYS CHANGING

It seemed to me, and it still does, that the same is likely to be true of religious and philosophical beliefs. Philosophy has changed from the times of Plato and Aristotle, and it has produced Thomism, existentialism, rationalism, empiricism, dualism, idealism, and materialism, to name but a few. If philosophy is, as Whitehead said, a set of footnotes to Plato, the footnotes are now much longer than the text. It takes a certain arrogance and myopia to think that any of these are completely true, and that there is nothing further to be said. We will probably be attracted to one or more of them to a large extent, whether or not that is due to our potty-training. But we will probably want to make our own adjustments to them, adjustments that may be either stupid or interesting, or possibly both.

Why should the same not be true of religious beliefs? If so, nothing that was said thousands of years ago will be acceptable today just as it stands. We may be attracted to one or more of them, but we will make our own adjustments, and not expect ever to be completely right.

Admittedly some believers will say, "No, the truth as been revealed once and for all, in this book or by this teacher, and we must simply repeat it for ever." I think anybody who has studied philosophy or science will have trouble believing this. I certainly have trouble believing it. That was probably why people at my theological college thought I was not 'sound.' But I was now more encouraged to think that it was they who had Christianity wrong.

If we look at the range of religions in the world, what is called inspiration or revelation seems to be a response to personal experiences and reflections that are inspired by a presence and power beyond either us or our cultural environment. It is, or seems to be, an apprehension of some transcendent presence. But there is no reason to think the apprehension should be inerrant or complete. It will carry with it all the presuppositions and many of the limitations of our culture and personality.

There are two main arguments that influence this view. First, it puts religion in the same boat as science, morality, politics, philosophy, and art. In each area, human knowledge changes as experiences and reflections change. There are some things in each area that we may be sure of. Yet there are many things that change over the years. Humans do not in general ever have complete knowledge. They develop and learn—though unfortunately they may also wither and forget. That is as likely to be true in religion as anywhere else.

Second, the view helps to explain how people can differ so much about what revelation is, and who has it. Religions differ greatly, and even within religion new sects arise. My own church, the Church of England, split off from the Roman Catholic Church, partly because King Henry VIII had trouble with his sex life. At the present time there are three parts of the C of E that rarely speak to each other—conservative evangelicals, Anglo-Catholics, and a liberal or 'open' group, which is so open that it cannot even agree on what to call itself. If Christian religion really was about a changeless and inerrant set of instructions from God, surely we would all know what those instructions were. Annoyingly for conservatives, the instructions are so unclear that believers differ completely about what they say, and about who, if anyone, has the authority to tell everyone else what they say. The obvious solution (it seems to me) is to admit that there are no clear instructions, written or otherwise, and we just have to say that people experience and interpret their revelations from a transcendent source in personal and varying ways.

This thought is encouraged by the doctrine, common to many religions, that the transcendent source is actually unknowable and incomprehensible. Once you say that, you can never claim to be sure that what you apprehend is what you think it is, since then it would be knowable.

Is this the end of religion? It is the end of a certain sort of religion, the sort that depends on having a changeless and complete body of knowledge delivered direct from God (or whatever the relevant transcendent reality is). If a religion claims an extraordinary apprehension of God, interpreted in provisional and partial terms, that is OK. That is precisely what many Christians say about the Old Testament revelation. To be consistent, they should say it about the New Testament, and therefore about themselves, as well.

CAMBRIDGE THEOLOGICAL DISPUTES, GYPS, AND MARROW SPOONS

There was a well-known very radical theologian, Don Cupitt, the dean of Emmanuel College, in Cambridge, who wrote a book called *Taking Leave of God* (1980). He and I ran joint seminars, in which we debated various ideas of God and various interpretations of religious belief. We got on very well, but I decided, in order to get these friendly debates into the public arena, to write a polemical response, which I called *Holding Fast to God* (1982). We were really two slightly radical philosophical theologians debating the rather abstruse issue of whether the word 'God' named an entity or was used to express commitments to a way of life. The press got wind of this and turned it into some sort of heroic battle for traditional Christian faith against the army of unbelievers. I was named 'the defender of the faith,' and Don was a disciple of Satan. Given my own history, this was rather ironic. However, it was a lesson on how subtle and friendly discussions can be turned into fierce fights that arouse violent passions and even hatreds. Especially on religious issues, it is vital both to see the weaknesses of human understanding, and the importance of kindness and tolerance.

While at Trinity Hall, I gave the Edward Cadbury Lectures at Birmingham, which I published in 1984 as *Rational Theology and the Creativity of God*. This is a statement of the view of God that I was later to develop in more detail. It sees God as a dynamic, creative, power realising the divine nature as love by the creation of other persons, relating to them in new responsive ways, and aiming to bring them to fulfilment by union with the divine life. Though long out of print, it stands as an early statement of what I was later to term personal idealism.

At Cambridge I was able to interact with scientists and philosophers, believing and unbelieving. That is one of great advantages of a university, particularly in a college where experts in different disciplines are forced to eat together, and can interact and come to a wider and more nuanced view of the human condition.

That is the theory, anyway. I must admit, however, that it is not always so. Colleges are famous for the intensity of the quarrels over the most trivial topics that can be imagined. Many years ago, the fellows, who were all men, had to sit in terms of their seniority (i.e., how long they had been fellows) at dinner, which they were expected to attend. They had to sit next to the same persons at dinner every night for life. At first this was very pleasant. But after twenty years or so, conversation began to run low. In the worst case, one was left with four or five silent old men at one end of high table glaring at one another as they tried to remember what they had once been famous for. Whereas they had once discussed the possibilities of finding cures for cancer, when they spoke, they now discussed the possibilities of getting a new pair of false teeth.

Things are different now, of course. My own college, Trinity Hall, admitted women in the year I was appointed to a fellowship. At my interview, I know a decision about this matter had just been taken, but I did not know what it was. I confess that I said, "Well, on the one hand, . . . but on the other hand." But I was wearing a trendy leather jacket, so it was plain what I really thought—I was later told that wearing that jacket helped to get me the job. Such are the ways to academic success.

Philosopher a la mode (1970)

Cambridge colleges even then were very peculiar institutions. We dined very well, with some of the best wines in the world; we had a college butler; and I had a gyp (the Cambridge word for a college servant)—oddly, in view of my past, of Arabic descent—who was even prepared to make up a fire for me in my rather impressive set of rooms, complete with bathroom and bedroom, with portraits of worthy gentlemen and their coats of arms, with whom of course I had no connection, hanging on the walls. He was wise enough, however, to ask me if I would prefer a nice gas fire, and I, being new to Cambridge and its ways, said that would be very nice. I think I would have felt uncomfortable at the thought of him carrying buckets of coal up the stairs to my rooms each morning, but I did not mind him switching on the gas fire.

In fact, I was married, as were most of the fellows, and rarely used the bedroom, except after particularly riotous termly college feasts at which senior members had to try to keep the Boat Club in order (an impossible task). Marriage had become quite acceptable, even though it had been viewed with horror as a dangerous innovation by an earlier generation. Even so, college life often proceeded as though the fellows were all single. I recall that fellows were not allowed to invite their wives to college feasts—one comment by a member of another college, was, "Who would want to sit next to a wife?" But the fellows of my college certainly did not agree with that, and I also recall that at Trinity Hall we asked each other's wives to college feasts instead.

So my job pushed me firmly into the ranks of the privileged. Yet most of us had very little actual money. I think the assumption was that we had private means, which was not in general true, and which was certainly not true in my case. We were a sort of impoverished middle class, who lived very well as long as we neglected our families. We could dine on caviar and champagne, while our wives had scrambled egg on toast with the children.

Fellows took turns at carrying out the annual inspection of the college silver (during the English Civil War, the college had written to Oliver Cromwell, saying, "We heartily support thy cause; and please send back the college silver." Which he did, so it was a fine collection). My turn came, and I went down to the college cellars with the butler. He picked up some strange spoons with very long handles and tiny spoon bits at the end. "Do you know, sir," he said, "Some of the younger fellows do not even know what these are." "That is very sad," I responded, not having the slightest idea what they were for. Later on, I looked these objects up in a book (Google did not exist in those days, and people still read books), and found out that they were marrow spoons, for extracting marrow from bones at college feasts. My time at Glasgow and King's College, London had failed to teach me this, and I had never been to a real public school.

TRAVELLING ABROAD—INDIA

While at Cambridge, I was appointed to the Teape Lectureship, which involved a visit to a number of places in India. The lecturer was required to read a hefty tome by Sri Aurobindo, and give talks on it to various Indian universities. However, when I got there, they said, "Please don't tell us any more about Sri Aurobindo. We are fed up with all that. Tell us about Cambridge. Did you ever meet Wittgenstein?" Nevertheless, I found out a great deal about many Indian types of philosophy and religion, and also a great deal about travelling on Indian trains. This was, for a European, an alarming experience, and involved sharing a wooden bench for five hours with two or three Indian families, all of whom had apparently booked the same seat, next to a hole in the floor which turned out to be the public convenience. And that was first class! Most passengers seemed to be sitting outside on the carriage roof, which was considerably less smelly, though rather more draughty. I learned too late that I should have booked air-conditioned trains.

Eating involved some of the most delicious and elaborate vegetarian meals I have ever encountered, but, at the other end of the scale were such delicacies as hen's feet and offal soup (I think it was soup; it was certainly offal.) Being interested in Indian religion, I asked if I could visit some ashrams, and meet some genuine Hindu holy men. I was given a guide, but knowing that I was a Christian priest, they gave me a guide who turned out to be an Indian bishop. He was a lovely man, but perhaps not the right person to take me to Hindu ashrams. We slept on stone floors in the ashrams, and each night the bishop would kneel down and pray. And each night he would conclude the prayers by saying, "Finally, O Lord, we pray that this ashram might fall down in the night. Amen." He was not the best exponent of inter-religious dialogue.

I particularly looked forward to a meeting with some inhabitants of Nagaland who were going to give a concert at a hall in Calcutta. Nagaland was at that time a vast territory in Northeast India, closed to foreign visitors, and was the home of tribal peoples who had been head-hunters until very recently. Being interested in indigenous cultures and customs, I was expecting to see men in tribal costumes performing some of their sacred dances. What turned up, however, was a group of young men in blue jeans, wielding not battle-axes but guitars, and singing, "There is a happy land far, far away . . ." It turned out that some Southern Baptists from the USA had secretly flown into Nagaland by helicopter and converted the nation, who were all now Southern Baptists, with a large and impressive Baptist cathedral. I suppose it was better than head-hunting.

I must say, I loved India. I loved the smells, the colours, and the vibrancy, the hills, the plains, the songs, and the temple rituals. Yet the extreme poverty of those who lived among piles of rubbish while others could spend millions of rupees on a wedding feast was depressing, Seeing these things, my wife, who was often with me, said, "I could not bear to come here again." But when we got back to Cambridge, after a month or two, she began to say, "I must go back to India." We did, and soon we were completely captivated by that diverse and complex country. The British have, of course, a very ambiguous relationship to India, as it was once the jewel in the crown of the British Empire. Since I was not myself part of the governing elite of Britain, or of its more exploitative trading practices, I was not inclined to identify myself with colonialist ideas. But I had to admit that there were things about our past history of which we should be ashamed. It was clear to me, however, that there were many positive aspects of the encounter of British and Indian cultures. Not least was the interaction of philosophical ideas, which led to fascinating and exciting developments of thought, as the great historical traditions of Indian philosophy became better known in the West, and Western ideas often re-energised and modified ancient Indian traditions. There were, of course, misunderstandings on both sides, but also the birth of more creative understandings—and naturally, of special interest to me, the impact of Indian forms of idealism on European thought. The country, too, casts a spell from which, once cast, it is impossible to escape. As a professor of religion, I know that there is no such thing as Hinduism, as the term, invented by the Portuguese, covers many different forms of belief. That may be so, but I still have a great affection for it. I even called myself a 'Christian Hindu' for a while, but I found that neither Christians nor Hindus believed me.

CHRISTIAN VEDANTA

Perhaps I should explain that a little. There are many religious movements in India, but one of them is Vedanta, (technically, a commentary on the Veda and Upanishads, the main Indian holy texts), which is a rather philosophically inclined movement, and so appealed to me. There are twelve main schools of Vedanta, but the one that attracted me is called *vishist-advaita,* qualified non-dualism, or the non-dualism of the differentiated (purists disagree about the best translation). Its founding father is Ramanuja, a twelfth-century sage. It accepts an ultimate non-dualism—everything that exists is part of one all-embracing reality—but within it there is a Supreme Lord, and then there are many souls, and the material world, which together form the 'body' of the Lord. This is sometimes called 'the Methodism of India,' because it emphasises the importance of loving devotion to the Supreme Lord. It is also strangely like the Christian belief that the church is the 'body' of Christ, and that all things will finally be united in Christ—both central New Testament claims.

The best-known movement in the West, which owes much to Ramanuja, is popularly known as the Hare Krishnas, who process around the streets singing "Hare Krishna" and banging drums. This may seem like a curious Western sect—and it is. But it is a Westernised version of a major and respected Indian tradition.

I like Ramanuja's teaching very much and think there is much in it from which Christians can learn, which is why I sometimes called myself a Christian Hindu, or more precisely, a Christian Vedantin. Many of my friends pointed out that Hindus believe in reincarnation, whereas Christians do not. Surely, they said, these are just incompatible. Christians do not expect to be reborn as potatoes, after all.

But it is not so simple. Reincarnation is just a word for the embodiment of a mind in another body, and that is exactly what St. Paul meant when he said that we are resurrected in spiritual, not physical, bodies (1 Corinthians 15:44). Gregory of Nyssa, a great orthodox theologian, wrote that after death we may have a succession of different, hopefully more glorious, bodies, as we approach more nearly the knowledge of the glory of God. That is reincarnation—not on this earth, to be sure, but in realms of being beyond this spacetime. Hindus speak of being reborn in more spiritual realms too, so there is not all that much difference. They do not seriously expect to become potatoes—what would be the point, since potatoes would not even know that they were people who had turned into potatoes. They do not ask, "What have I done to become a potato?" and then remember that it is because they had been a very bad person in their last lives. It was now up to them to become very good potatoes, in order to get a better incarnation next time.

There is room for convergence between these great traditions, if only people can get over some of the more popular, superstitious, and pre-scientific ideas that tend to litter religious life. Unfortunately, many Christians cannot rid themselves of the idea that Hindus are polytheists, and so cannot be believers in God. And many Hindus cannot rid themselves of the idea that Western Christians are not Indian, and so cannot be Hindus. I think they are both wrong, but I have given up trying to argue with them, and am content to let people call me what they like. I find that they do so anyway, and since they all disagree with each other, I will just leave them to it.

TRAVELLING ABROAD—ROMANIA

The oddest trip I made from Cambridge was not to India, but to Romania, a trip that happened, as has so often been the case with me, by mistake. The mistake was one of identity. A letter arrived at Trinity Hall one day from the patriarch of Romania inviting the dean to visit. The mistake was that the letter was meant for the archbishop of Canterbury, who had indeed been dean of Trinity Hall some time before me. Why it was sent to the dean, who was now me, I shall never know. But I was not one to miss a trip to such an exotic place.

I checked with the Foreign Office, and they pointed out that I had only been sent a one-way ticket, and advised me not to go. However, I went, and as I got out of the plane at Bucharest airport, I was astonished to see a red carpet and a big black limousine, together with the patriarch, waiting to greet me. As I descended from the plane, the patriarch looked very disappointed to see me. He had been expecting the distinguished Rt. Hon and Most Revd. Robert Runcie, and here was this unknown person using his plane ticket. I needed to think of some excuse rather quickly. "I am the archbishop's plenipotentiary," I said, not knowing quite what that meant, though I had heard the word somewhere. It turned out that they thought it meant that I was to be treated as though I was the archbishop, and I was. I walked through doors that only archbishops and patriarchs are allowed to walk through, and I spent a month making official visits to many monasteries and churches in Romania. When I got back, I told the archbishop what had happened, and he was kind enough to take it in good part, though he never made me his plenipotentiary again (not that he had done so the first time).

These visits involved drinking large amounts of tuica. (I do not know how to spell that, but it was pretty lethal. After a few glasses, I no longer knew how to spell anything. The amounts were individually quite small, but had to be swallowed in one gulp, and over a day's visits they had a major effect.) At that time, it was said that about half the clergy were in fact members of the Securitate, the secret communist police force that reported on everyone else. Nobody knew who they were exactly, but I reckoned that they had a very hard time sitting through hours of Orthodox liturgies, and groaning quietly to themselves while the genuine monks prayed at great length.

I was asked to give some talks at various universities about Western and Eastern churches, which was not at all my field of expertise, though I was not in a position to refuse. To make it worse, I often had to speak in German, which both I and my audiences only half-understood, so most of the finer points of my expositions were lost. At first, I got little reaction to my laboured speeches (I find that making jokes in German, or at least in my version of German, produces catastrophic results).

But one day, as if by chance, I mentioned the name of Maximus the Confessor, and the audience began to clap. Evidently this ancient theologian, who is very important in the Eastern Orthodox churches, though largely unknown in the West, meant a lot to them. Tentatively, I tried saying, "As Maximus the Confessor said, . . ." and the audience got more and more enthusiastic. Vastly encouraged, I just added to virtually every sentence, "I agree with Maximus . . . ," and soon they were all standing and applauding loudly. From that time on, my talks were a great success, though I doubt if the secret police knew what I was talking about. I actually doubt if *anyone* knew what I was talking about, but whatever it was, I was supporting Maximus, and I suspect this had something to do with how the church really felt about the government that was repressing them, infiltrating their monasteries and official church leadership, and indeed destroying Romania as a viable country.

At that time Romania was run by Nicolae Ceausescu, a vicious dictator, and the Rumanian Orthodox Church was firmly in his grip. There were those in the church put in place by the president who were there merely to carry out his orders. But there were many heroic souls, who tried to work, largely in secret, for justice and genuine concern for the poor. The trouble was that one could never be sure which were which. I became great friends with the person who acted as my interpreter, and he seemed very genuine. Yet when I returned to England, I was told that he was probably a government agent. Dictatorship destroys all trust and friendship, and it is not uncommon even for children to report their parents to the authorities. People in countries like Britain may complain about our government, but at least we can get rid of it, and we can say what we really think without being tortured. I just could not get the Romanians to believe that the British government had no interest in what I was saying. They really believed that what I said was something I had been told to say. Though why anyone in the British government would be interested in discourses on Maximus the Confessor I have no idea.

KING'S COLLEGE, LONDON, 1983–1986

I GREATLY ENJOYED MY time at Cambridge, but while I lived a very privileged life in college, I was also working pretty hard, being a dean and student counsellor, teaching and lecturing in the university, sitting on various college committees, being in charge of a student residence, and trying to do some research. I reckoned that seven years was about as long as I could do all these things at the same time. Also, because of some peculiar ideas I have about education, we wanted the children to go to schools in London. The professor who had been so difficult had now retired from King's. So I applied to be the F. D. Maurice Professor of Moral and Social Theology at King's London, and I gather I did rather well at my interview. This was because just before the interview I had been on a television programme (the studio was just over the river Thames from King's), and in those days they served lots of alcohol to people who appeared on TV. This was apparently because it was good for viewing numbers. Consequently, I turned up at the interview rather drunk, and I have no idea what I said. Whatever it was, I was appointed, no doubt to the great and justified annoyance of the more sober candidates, and found myself immersed in the world of medical ethics and all the debates about gender and death that were getting more and more complex every day.

Moving back to London was a bit of a shock. In Cambridge we had lived in a college house that was rather spacious. We even had a croquet lawn, which was shared with the students, but when they were on vacation, which they seemed to be for most of the year, it was all ours. As a new London professor, I found that the most we could afford anywhere near King's was a small cupboard next to a railway line. However, we searched assiduously, and we eventually found a very dilapidated house in Kew Gardens, just by the Victoria gate. We could afford it for two reasons: It was so dilapidated that a television company used it for a film about a bankrupted banker and paid us for the privilege. And it was under the direct flight path to Heathrow Airport, so that the house shook as Concorde (remember that?) passed overhead. It apparently used our house as the place to lower its landing gear and go into reverse thrust, which made conversation impossible and caused our hair to stand on end twice a day. Also, that was a time when banks offered to lend alarmingly large sums of money that we could not possibly repay. I remember one bank offering to lend us a million pounds, which I had never seen in all my life. I took out a mortgage for a lot less than that, and as it turned out, inflation was so high that after some years the loan began to seem really quite small. It is hard to remember those years. The house just went on increasing in value, as it has done since we sold it, so much so that we could not now afford to buy it back again.

MORALITY AND THE BIBLE

As the F. D. Maurice Professor, I became a director of the King's College Centre for Medical Ethics and was introduced to the rapidly changing world of medicine, and all the major ethical problems it involved. At least here was a place where philosophy might help to make a practical difference. I was very heartened to see the way in which the discussion of ethical problems was now part of medical training. Things were not always like that. When a national survey was taken, asking whether medical ethics was part of medical training courses, all the university medical faculties said, "Yes, of course," while all the doctors who had been trained there said, "No; what is that?" As a matter of fact, the pressure for training in medical ethics came largely from nurses, not doctors. It is nurses who have to deal with many of these problems in practice. There are huge moral differences about such subjects as abortion, patient's autonomy of choice, and euthanasia. What is needed is a place to discuss these things calmly and reasonably, and to find the best reasons for one's own beliefs. That is the only thing that can distinguish rational commitment from prejudice.

In addition, now that I was a professor of moral theology, everybody began to think that I was some sort of spokesman for the Anglican Church—everybody, that is, except the bishops of the Anglican Church, who continued to regard theology professors as dangerous radicals, bent on destroying the faith. Nevertheless, I became a member of the Anglican Board for Social Responsibility. This is a body that produces thousands of pages of moral advice every year, and sends it to clergy around the country, though I have never met anyone who has actually read them.

One reason for this is that members of the board disagree with each other so much that the moral advice offered is almost impossible to discover. There are some things that are generally agreed, but even they are liable to change within a few years. Artificial contraception, for example, was condemned at the beginning of the twentieth century as frustrating the purpose of sexual intercourse. But in just a few years it was apparently 'discovered' that one purpose of intercourse was to express love, and that God did not necessarily want people to have as many babies as possible, so contraception was approved—within limits. The limits were not as strict as St. Jerome had suggested, who accepted sexual intercourse, but said that it was sinful to find it pleasant. The Church of England, always priding itself on taking 'the middle way,' accepted a certain degree of pleasure, but not too much, and thought that two or three babies (plus a dog) per couple was the number that God was most likely to approve of. Nowadays it is almost impossible to hear an Anglican priest preaching on contraception at all. One member of the General Synod (a sort of governing body) even gave a speech in which she said that she had been masturbating for years, and it seemed perfectly natural to her. I suppose that is a very effective method of contraception.

Churches have always had problems about sex and marriage. Even in the 1950s divorced people were not allowed to take Communion, and kings had to abdicate if they married divorced persons. Yet King Henry VIII, who more or less 'started' the Church of England and called himself the head of it, was very keen not only on divorce, but on beheading some of his wives, which would seem rather extreme these days, even if it was an undoubtedly effective method of separation. If you look to the Bible for guidance, it is not much help. You are likely to find that polygamy was favoured (Solomon had seven hundred wives, and three hundred concubines, and nobody complained—though I do not suppose anyone consulted the wives—see 1 Kings 11:13), concubines and slaves were allowed, and even in the New Testament women had to obey their husbands and keep quiet in church, with their heads covered in case anyone got over-excited.

I suppose there are still people who approve of all this, but most have definitely moved on. It is hard to think that God has changed his mind, so we must accept that we have changed our moral views since biblical times. We longer think that women should be subordinate to men, that we can

71

keep slaves, and that all political leaders are appointed by God (including Nero, Stalin, and Hitler), and we must obey them, even though all these things are clearly stated in the Bible. To put it bluntly, the Bible can get it wrong in matters of morality, so we can no longer justify our moral views by simply quoting bits of the Bible. That is perhaps why bishops regard theology professors as dangerous radicals.

Where, then, can we get our moral views from? Despite what I have said about the Bible, there are bits of it that give a clue. One is that "the entire law is summed up in a single command, 'love your neighbour as yourself'" (Galatians 5:14). The other is the statement that "we serve in the new way of the Spirit, and not in the old way of the written code" (Romans 7:6). Both these statements are by St. Paul. They are usually neglected by self-proclaimed Bible-based moralists, who take the words of St. Paul about sex, slaves, the submission of women, and supine obedience to authority, as a new written code that must be obeyed. In doing so, they misunderstand Paul, completely contradicting what he was trying to say about written laws, and so they are not really Bible-based at all.

This does not mean that we can believe what we want. It means that we must work out for ourselves what caring for the well-being of others requires. That is 'the way of the Spirit,' the way of universal compassion and kindness. Well, that is what I thought. Most people expected me to defend the ancient traditions of the church. But it seemed to me that most of these traditions had been invented fairly recently, especially in the Church of England, where it only takes thirty years for something to be regarded as an ancient tradition. In such circles, the best argument against doing something is that it has never been done before. As Lord Wellington said, "Reform, reform! Aren't things bad enough already?"

MAKING MORAL DECISIONS

Remembering my years as a moral philosopher, I remembered that in moral matters, there are indeed some things that are pretty basic, like caring for others, not being selfish, and seeking to bring out the positive potentialities in people. But there are many other things that fail the test of universal concern for all living beings (are they not our neighbours?), things like cruelty to animals, thinking my country or family should always come first, or be specially privileged, or trying to be rich or famous whatever the cost to others. Traditions, however ancient, must be tested against the criterion of practical concern for the well-being of all. If our moral beliefs fail this test, or if they are based on believing some Bible texts (like "do not get divorced") and ignoring others (like "love your enemies") they must be changed. It is pretty obvious to me that, while a loving marriage is a great good and should be promoted as much as possible, chaining together for life two people who hate each other, while preventing them from seeking a more loving relationship with someone else, is not seeking the well-being of anyone. It is similarly obvious to me that if two people of the same sex wish to commit themselves to caring for one another exclusively, loyally, and faithfully, for life, that is something that should be welcomed and embraced.

However, I found there were people who would rather carry on un-critically obeying a rule that was proposed thousands of years ago by a member of a Middle Eastern polygamous, concubine-and-slave-owning, patriarchal, and sometimes genocidal society. We have all been there, but most of us, Jewish and gentile, have moved on considerably. Moral views have changed, in the world and in the church, and it is a good thing that they should go on changing, where the rule of love is broken.

MORE ABOUT SEX

Many religions, especially in the Abrahamic tradition, seem to have a fixa-tion with sex. For a start, they are very patriarchal. Men are seen as superior to women. According to the Bible, Eve was made out of Adam's rib, and therefore women need to keep quiet in church, and obey their husbands. It is hard to see how these conclusions follow from what is obviously a legend, or why anyone should take the legend literally in the first place. Does any-one seriously believe that women are made out of the bones of a man? Or does anyone believe that angels might get aroused if women did not wear hats in church (1 Corinthians 1:10)?

The fact is that the reasons given for male superiority are pretty stupid. They are based on nothing more than prejudice, and they completely un-dermine Paul's teaching, elsewhere, that in Christ there is neither male nor female (Galatians 3:28). In which case, we have to say that some specific bits of the Bible are incompatible with the fundamental religious percep-tion that all beings are of concern to God, and that we should care for the well-being of everyone, whatever their race or sex. Which means that we should love them as we love ourselves, not as inferiors or as something less than us.

Once you have got that far, and you look at what the Bible says about the relations of men and women, you are bound to think that it is probably going to express the prejudices of a patriarchal society, not a direct order from God. And so it is. In the Hebrew Bible, polygamy is taken for granted—as I have mentioned, Solomon had seven hundred wives. Having concubines was also regarded as normal, but they were slaves, and so did not count. Even in the New Testament, slavery is never condemned, and slaves are told to obey their masters, even if their masters are cruel and tyrannical.

That throws doubt on the biblical passage usually quoted to support monogamy—that a man and a woman become "one flesh," and no one should split them up. Was Solomon one flesh with seven hundred women? Anyway, what does becoming "one flesh" mean? I suppose it means that two people are inseparably bound together in love. That is the intention of marriage, that two people mutually agree to live in trust, loyalty, fidelity, and care, for better or worse.

Does it mean that the two people must be of different sexes? Well, it is understandable that when women are pregnant and bear children, men should protect them in violent societies. And it is in the interests of mutual care that men should not continually be having affairs with other people, and conceiving babies they are not prepared to care for. There are good reasons for monogamy, and it had become generally accepted by Jesus' time—though it is never explicitly commanded in the New Testament, except that it is recommended for bishops.

But that does not mean that mutual trust, loyalty, fidelity, and care can only exist between people of different sexes, or that people of the same sex cannot promise to live in such a union for better or worse.

We know that St. Paul did not approve of gay and lesbian relationships. He called them unnatural and shameful (Romans 1:26–32). But we already know that Paul did not approve of men with long hair or women without hats, and we don't take much notice of that. The question of what is natural is a difficult one. It could be just describing what people do most of the time, or what usually happens. The trouble is that people tell lies and boast most of the time. Even if you have sex, you do not produce babies most of the time, and some people are unable to have babies. Are they unnatural? They might be unusual, but there is nothing wrong with being unusual. It is unusual to be a philosopher, so I suppose being a philosopher is unnatural, but I am rather proud of that.

Some sexual practices are shameful—having sex with children is shameful, because it is apt to harm the child. Having sex with someone against their will is harmful. Having sex with donkeys—I am not sure about that, but it shows a certain lack of taste.

Whatever is the case with donkeys, sexual acts between human persons are connected with love and respect for personality. Sexual acts should be expressions of love. Christian churches have not always been clear about this. The 1662 Anglican marriage service declared that marriage is primarily for the procreation of children. It is also for those "who have not the gift of continency," so that they can keep themselves undefiled. Only in third place comes the admission that it might be for "the mutual society, help, and comfort" of the married couple—and even that makes no mention that sexual activity might express love. It makes marriage sound more like a meeting of Alcoholics Anonymous than like a romantic liaison.

Of course, it is important that children should be raised in loving homes. And, of course, romantic passion alone is not enough to keep a marriage going. But it is worth supporting and encouraging life-long commitments to fidelity and love between persons, whatever gender they may acknowledge.

Could the church bless such commitments? Well, I have a prayerbook for priests at home, and it includes a prayer of blessing for "anything whatsoever." I have known that to cover submarines and armed forces, so I expect it would cover gays and lesbians with no difficulty.

But would that be a marriage? Even in the most conservative Christian traditions, priest do not 'make' marriages; they are not the 'ministers of the sacrament.' The couple themselves do that; the priest simply blesses the union in the name of God. Therefore, the Christian answer should be, "Yes, if a couple want their union to be blessed by God, that is a marriage, whether or not they both (or neither) have testicles."

Unfortunately, Christian churches remain completely divided on this issue. The irony is that I do not even regard it as a religious issue. It has nothing to do with relating to a higher spiritual reality and seeking positive human relationships of goodness. Unless, that is, you think that only those who order their sexual lives in a specific way (or, in some religions, who have no sexual lives at all) are permitted to have such a relationship to spiritual reality.

All this is just to explain why I side with the attitude of the American Episcopal Church on these issues and consider myself an American

Episcopalian (as well as a Hindu), even if no-one else does. For some years, I have had a close association with the Virginia Theological Seminary, which even, in a spirit of extreme generosity, gave me an honorary doctorate. While the seminary is a very inclusive international body, and accepts candidates of many different shades of opinion, it is, like most of the American Episcopal Church, firmly committed to the acceptance of gay and lesbian relationships.

In my own small bit of the church, the Church of England, I am told that the mind of the church has not yet decided on this issue and forbids me to preside at marriages of gays and lesbians. However, I doubt whether the Church of England has a mind. It seems to be run by people just like me, who meet in committees and take a vote, which happens to be wrong on quite a lot of issues, including this one. As a matter of fact, in the 1960s, when I was a participant in a working party of the Advisory Council for the Church's Ministry, which produced *Teaching Christian Ethics* (1974), a guide for theological colleges, I held these views then; it hardly new. As for me, I shall continue to be prepared to support and preside at gay marriages, while explaining that they are not marriages but blessings, while at the same time making it clear that marriages are nothing but blessings. That is, I tell myself, a characteristic Anglican compromise.

ABSOLUTE MORAL RULES AND HUMAN WELL-BEING

I am not suggesting that it is easy to decide what the principle of compassionate and enduring love requires, or that this is the only moral rule one should follow. But I do think it is the most fundamental principle of morality. It is at this point that I find myself in disagreement with many moral stances officially taken by the Roman Catholic Church. Catholic moral theologians, including Pope John Paul II, have held that there are absolute moral rules that can never be broken in any circumstances (see the papal encyclical *Veritatis Splendor* [1993]). Thus, it can never be permitted to lie, steal, or kill in *any* situation, however critical. I believe this to be incompatible with genuine care for the well-being of others. I would not hesitate to lie to save a life in a critical situation. I would not hesitate to steal from the rich to save someone from starvation. And I would not hesitate to kill to save a person from prolonged and terminal agony.

Catholic theologians have coined the phrase 'the culture of death' to cover the latter sort of case, and it has been an effective and memorable slogan. I would prefer to speak of a 'culture of compassion.' The point is that moral rules can sometimes conflict—'Do not lie' can conflict with 'Do not permit someone to be unjustly killed,' and 'Do not kill the innocent' can conflict with 'Relieve acute pain if it is untreatable and terminal.' In such cases, the rule that is held to be more stringent should prevail. This is to say that no specific moral rules are absolute; they are *prima facie* rules, or 'other things being equal' rules.

Such decisions are always hard, and they should only be made in rare and critical conditions. But such conditions do occur, and I have come across them myself. In my view, cases like the abortion of a foetus after rape, or medical procedures directly intending to end the life of a terminally ill or injured person, are among those that raise genuine moral conflicts, basically between respect for human life, and compassion for human pain and suffering. This is not at all like saying that in some cases moral rules can simply be ignored. But it is saying that there are genuine moral conflicts, and when they occur, what one takes to be the strongest rule should prevail. The nearest thing to an absolute is love and compassion, and what that suggests in particular cases can be very difficult and even agonising to work out. Moral decision-making is not easy, but appeal to absolute moral rules can be brutal and inhumane, when it ignores the question of what makes for true human well-being.

NUCLEAR WEAPONS AND CAVIAR

The world has changed greatly since biblical times, and some of our greatest moral problems were not even imagined then. One of them is the possession and use of nuclear weapons. I inevitably got involved in that debate. I was sent, this time officially by the Church of England, to Moscow to participate in a conference about weapons of mass destruction. Even though it was official, I was still free to say what I thought, though it became very clear to me that the purpose of the conference, organised by Russia, was to get the Western churches to use their influence to demilitarise the European states bordering the Soviet Union. Russian weapons were to remain in place, of course, to preserve the security of the peace-loving Russians. But the West's weapons had to be removed, as they were evidence of the aggressive intentions of the fiendish West. I felt there was a flaw in this logic somewhere. I remember that I made a very rude speech, pointing this out, and that was the end of my diplomatic career. The only good thing about the whole affair was that we were all taken for a boat ride down the Volga and fed on mounds of Beluga caviar, courtesy of the Moscow patriarchate (more accurately known as the KGB Bible study group).

KING'S COLLEGE, LONDON, 1986–1991

BACK TO PHILOSOPHY

HAVING ESTABLISHED MYSELF AS a dangerous radical, I was rather relieved when the chair of the history and philosophy of religion at King's College became vacant, and I was invited to move into it. I could then revert to tackling problems that no one else was interested in, and out of the limelight of perpetual and public controversy. It was a cowardly decision in a way, but I really was more interested in metaphysical questions, and I thought I had probably done all I could to establish a particular position in moral theology and could leave to others the extremely complex and detailed studies needed to discover what truly makes for human well-being.

In my new role I became the head of the Department of Religious Studies, a Bachelor of Arts degree that studied religion, not just Christian theology. The study of religion, rather like philosophy, usually begins with a course that explains that nobody can define what 'religion' is, so we are not quite sure what it is that we are going to be studying. When I say that nobody can define it, I am aware that many people have tried, but few people have agreed with what they said.

In the United States, teaching in college departments of religion often requires that teachers have no religious beliefs—this is to ensure impartial treatment. All religions can be treated equally, because they are all wrong. Theology is often siphoned off into special departments for the training of clergy. These are more sympathetic to religion, though they sometimes hold that one religion is right and all the others are wrong.

In the UK this is not the case. Theology and religious studies are usually merged. It is not assumed that only one religion is right, but both teachers and students may have any religious beliefs or none. When I was at King's there was a BD in theology and a BA in religious studies. The former was focussed on Christianity, but was very popular with atheists and agnostics, who often found that they believed more than the Christians did. The latter was taught by psychologists, anthropologists, sociologists, philosophers, Hindus, Buddhists, Muslims, and me. The students were from many different backgrounds, but included a surprising number of pagans and witches, though we tended to draw the line at accepting Satanists. I myself had many Muslim and Hindu graduate students, from Pakistan, Turkey, and India, who have gone on to distinguished careers in their home countries.

DEFINING RELIGION

This variety demonstrated why we could not define religion. Religions all believed such very different things. 'God' was only one option amongst many, and the range of possible choices seemed limitless. However, having said that religion cannot be defined, here is my definition. It is a stipulative definition (meaning that is how I propose to use the word, whatever anybody else thinks):

> *There exists a spiritual reality, it can be known by human beings,*
> *some human beings seem to have particularly acute awareness of it,*
> *and conscious relation to it can improve the quality of human life.*

This has to be a very broad definition, if it is to cover many religions, and there will be borderline cases. At a previous survey of religious affiliation in the UK, some people classified themselves as Jedi Knights. Did they belong to a religion? On my definition, I suppose we would have to say, Yes. The spiritual reality is the Force, Jedi Knights have special access to it, and watching *Star Wars* films can make people feel much happier. The main problem is that the whole thing was just made up in Hollywood by people who would probably not regard themselves as spiritually advanced, but wanted to make a lot of money. Some people would think that all religions are rather like that, though that seems unduly cynical.

What about soccer? Vast crowds sing hymns, make pilgrimages to see the ritual of placing a ball into a sacred net, worship their favourite players, and treasure holy relics, such as old balls and smelly T-shirts. This is rather like a religion, but it seems to lack the dimension of supra-material reality—although a committed Platonist might say that the ideal soccer game does exist beyond space and time, and all actual soccer matches are just faint shadows of this timeless reality.

What about Buddhism? Some people think that Buddhism is not a religion, because it does not believe in God. Actually, most Buddhists believe in more gods than Christians do, but none of them created the universe. Nevertheless, Buddhists wear special robes, live in monasteries, light candles and wave incense around, and gather together to recite passages of scripture in carefully choreographed ways. This looks like a religion, but more to the point, it has a non-physical reality, *nirvana*, which was accessed by the Buddha in a special way, and access to it is said to deliver people from suffering and death. That seems to be a very good religion.

If you accept a definition of this sort, the contrast often made by people who say they are 'spiritual but not religious' collapses. If the spiritual is something that is not a physical entity in spacetime, if there are teachers or guides who seem to have experienced it, and if getting into contact with it is life-enhancing, that *is* a religion. I suppose what people mean by 'not being religious' is that they have not signed up to one of the 'big six' (approximately) major world religions, and prefer to mix and match their beliefs and practices from a range of sources.

THE CONFORMIST FALLACY

Mine may seem an unduly positive view of religion. But religions are after all meant to be positive and life-enhancing. Admittedly many forms of religion can be negative and life-suppressing, as Nietzsche notoriously held. But that is because they have let *people* into them. If there were no people in religions, religions would be much better. However, even though actual religions are full of argumentative and quarrelsome people, those who say that religions are the main causes of violence in the world have just forgotten their history lessons. Most groups who try to access a non-material reality to make life better are not primarily intending to cause violence, which obviously makes life worse. It is just that some people cannot get rid of their hatred of those who are different from them, and they think that religions are meant to make life better only for people who are like them. Most religions explicitly deny this, but somehow lots of religious believers forget to read those bits.

There are religious groups that persecute those who do not believe in their special understanding of spiritual reality. Believers in God have persecuted atheists, and people who disagree with them about what 'God' is. But this is a general human failing, and is not confined to the religious.

Atheists have also persecuted believers in God, and people who do not agree with them about how society should be run. It is nonsense to suppose that the Roman emperors were driven to conquer the world because of their religious beliefs, or that Stalin or Hitler were religious fanatics. They were fanatics, but what they were fanatical about was power, control, and domination of others.

What such fanatics have to do to religion is either to exterminate it or pervert it so that it becomes a way of selecting an elite group of superior people out of a general population of evil and dangerous enemies. The spiritual reality, they say, is only known by a select few, and all other views are to be abolished, by force, if necessary, because they actively oppose the truth.

This is the conformist fallacy, that disagreement entails hostility. If you do not agree with me, you are my enemy. The fallacy is found operative in politics, in morality, in religion, even in science. Politics is not by nature illiberal, but *in practice*, in the great empires and dictatorships of history, it is often repressive and intolerant. It is the same with religion. It would be ridiculous to say that politics was the cause of all violence. It is just as ridiculous to say that religion is.

AN EXPANSIVIST VIEW OF RELIGIONS

On the whole, learning about a range of religions tends to produce a greater sympathy with the diversity of the human condition, and a greater humility about the certainty of one's own commitments. After all, where so many people (almost everybody but oneself, it can seem) are wrong, and the arguments for differing views are so finely balanced, it is very unlikely that any one view is going to be the only one that is acceptable. It is much more likely that all religious views are going to be heavily influenced by the history and values of the culture in which they originate, and so are likely to change and develop as time goes on.

Since most people who write about God say, at some point, that God is beyond human understanding, this entails that nobody could understand God well enough to be absolutely sure that they are so obviously right that they should force other people to believe it. A decree of the Fourth Lateran Council (1215) of the Roman Catholic Church, speaking of God, states that "there is one highest, incomprehensible and ineffable reality," and then immediately goes on to describe the nature of God in painstaking detail. If a thing is *incomprehensible* and *ineffable*, how can anyone be so sure of what God is like? A little humility, not to say a little logical consistency, is called for!

Christianity, historically speaking, has found it difficult to accept that humans are not the centre of the universe. That has to change. It has often shown little concern for Jews, atheists, slaves, and animals. That has to change. It has filled many people with a crippling sense of guilt and a fear of what might happen after death. That has to change.

There should be no problem with changing. Humans are not the centre of the universe. Humility is supposed to be a Christian virtue, so to realise we are only tiny parts of a vast universe is a gain, not a loss. With regard to concern for others, humans should be concerned for all living things. Love, even of enemies, is the most basic Christian commandment, so it should not be hard to extend love to all conscious life. As for guilt, Christians above all should be free of guilt. If Jesus preached anything, it was that God forgives even the unjust, so that should get rid of guilt. He placed the Spirit of joy in his disciples, which questioned all rigid obedience to rules, especially if those rules frustrated human well-being.

I would argue that, since it seems that all religions are culturally influenced, and constantly change and develop, it is very unlikely that God (assuming there is one) would confine revelation to just one historical strand of belief, originating in the Middle East. There are many Indian traditions, East Asian traditions, and more localised indigenous traditions, too, which should be taken into account.

This suggests an 'expansivist' view of religions. We all start somewhere, either accepting a particular religious view or opposing that view. We can broaden our outlook by looking at other strands of human belief to see what they have to contribute to the idea of a life-enhancing encounter with spiritual reality—or, if there is no such reality, why so many have suffered from such a delusion for so long.

FOUR STRANDS OF RELIGIOUS THOUGHT

There are many strands of religious belief, but it is plausible to distinguish four main strands that have had different points of origin, and have been very influential in different parts of the world. In the Abrahamic or Middle Eastern strand, the spiritual reality is conceived as God, a personal being to whom one can relate in love and devotion. In at least one major Indian

Hindu strand, *Brahman* is the one reality of intelligence and bliss of which all things are parts. In a main Buddhist strand, *nirvana* is a state of bliss and compassion that is beyond any stain of personal individuality. In the East Asian strand, the *Tao* or the Way of Heaven is the path of harmony and balance that characterises an authentic human life.

There are more strands of religiosity than these, and these four contain sub-strands that reflect elements from other paths. The picture is very complex. It is even possible to combine them. Raimon Panikkar was a well-known scholar of religious studies who managed to be a Catholic priest, a Hindu priest, and a Buddhist monk at the same time. I once asked him if he believed in God, and he said, as a Christian, yes, but as a Buddhist, no. That is probably beyond most of us, but it is true that some immersion in different traditions can have a broadening and enriching effect on one's own beliefs and practices. If you don't like this, you call it syncretism. If you do, you call it wisdom.

MORE BOOKS

While I was at King's College, I wrote some books meant to be of general interest—*The Living God* (1984) was written primarily for the churches in which I helped out in Kew. *The Turn of the Tide* (1986) was originally a series on BBC radio, suggesting that materialism was on the way out, and spirituality was growing, a possibly over-optimistic thesis. Yet as religious adherence has declined, more people do seem to claim to be 'spiritual.' *Defending the Soul* (1992) took the same line, arguing that you could be an anti-materialist without being a Platonic dualist—and that Descartes was not the dualist he is supposed to be, but a supporter of a 'compound mind-body unity' view of human persons. *The Rule of Love* (1989) was an analysis of the 'sermon on the mount' in Matthew's Gospel. Then I had three slightly more weighty books (in my opinion, anyway): *Divine Action* (1990) tackled the question of how God could be said to act in the world, when scientists had apparently not noticed. *Images of Eternity* (1987), later re-titled *Concepts of God* (1998), surveyed how important members of major religious traditions speak about an ultimate and supremely valuable reality. I wrote about Sankara, Ramanuja (both Hindus, the latter being my own favourite), Buddhaghosa (Buddhist), Maimonides (Jewish), Al-Ghazzali (Muslim), and Aquinas (Catholic). Without underestimating the great differences between them, I claimed to find a certain convergence of beliefs about a supremely valuable and mind-like realm of spiritual being, which could be apprehended by humans. Knowledge of both the differences and convergences of these views would, I think, deepen and strengthen spiritual understanding. I would even go so far as to say, with Max Muller, the great Sanskrit scholar, that those who only understand one religion fail to understand it adequately.

This line of thought mostly arose from teaching religious studies to a very varied group of pagans, witches, Unitarians, Catholics, Mormons, Muslims, and humanists, which was an exciting if often confusing experience. Out of that teaching came a book, *A Vision to Pursue* (1991), which looked at religion as a global human phenomenon with many diverse facets but with important common ideals and commitments. The vision in question was to have a more global perspective on diverse faiths that could produce a wider and more mutually supportive spiritual understanding. If I were writing that book now, I would not put things in quite the same way, because it was written with my religious studies students in mind, who on the whole had a rather negative and over-simplified view of Christianity, and I tried to see things from their point of view. But it does represent a broad and generous attitude to world religions that I would still support.

ESCAPE TO THE COUNTRY

Kew was a wonderful place to live, with the magnificent botanic gardens not far from our door. The children thought it was wonderful too, mostly because it was not far from the Hammersmith Odeon, where famous pop groups used to play. The children could not afford to go to most of these concerts; it was enough for them that they were taking place nearby. But I worked at home much of the time, and I became increasingly irritated with living under the flight path to Heathrow. There was often a line of five or six planes visible in the sky at any one time, and roaring over my head all day. So we moved into the country, to Froyle, a village in Hampshire, a large and beautiful county to the South West of London, which was connected directly by rail with Waterloo, just over the River Thames from King's College, so that I could turn up at work from time to time.

There I again functioned as an honorary curate in a village church dedicated, rather remarkably for an Anglican church, to the Assumption of the Blessed Virgin. This was extremely 'high church,' with a statue of Mary in the nave, who always seemed to me suspiciously like the local goddess whose sacred hill was just behind the church. There I learned to soak people with holy water, suffocate them with incense, and make them process around the church for the slightest of pretexts. The congregation were not aware of how unusual this was in the Church of England. When there was a proposal to unite the church with another church on the other side of the hill, one member said, "I have never been over that hill, and I am not going to start now." This did not perhaps express a global view of religious life.

A BRUSH WITH BROADCASTING

As I have mentioned, King's was just over the river from a television studio, and next to Bush House, where the BBC World Service then was. I made a number of TV appearances, and did various talks, even a series or two, for the BBC. I was, as you might expect, put in the religious slot, where I discovered the true place of religion in British life. One day I was rung up by the BBC, and for some reason God was in the news (probably because some vicar had been up to no good). They wanted me to say something on the news, which would at last have convinced my mother that I was famous. But later that morning they rang again, and said, "Sorry; God has gone cold." That was the peak of my radio career.

At that time, the dean of King's College was Richard, now Lord, Harries, and he was a much more accomplished speaker than I was. Another moment of almost-fame for me came when I was having dinner at the Inns of Court with lots of judges and barristers. During the main course, a waiter came up and said, "Professor Ward, the BBC wants an urgent word with you." My social rating went up immediately, and I left the room to subdued murmurs of approval. When I got to the phone, a voice said, "This is really important. Have you got Richard Harries' phone number?" When I returned to the hall, I did not say what the urgent message had been—which increased my standing even more. It was obviously a state secret. I later found out that Richard and I were known by the TV people as 'Rent-a-Gob.' We could be found to make a religious comment on almost anything at short notice. But time-constraints were important. When we did "Thought for the Day" (a religious slot on Radio 4's weekday *Today* program) whatever we had to say had to be finished in time for the weather forecast, which I suspect was what people were really waiting to hear while they made the coffee. At least that gave me a good training in preaching short sermons, timed to within a few seconds. And it gave me a due appreciation of the

importance of religion. After speaking on *Woman's Hour* about capital pun-
ishment and the Old Testament, the presenter said, "Thank you so much,
Professor Ward. And now for the price of fish." It must have been one of
the most mysterious introductions to the price of fish ever to be broadcast.

RELIGION AND PHILOSOPHY AT SEA

After my astounding appearances on the media, I somehow found myself
engaged as a speaker on Swan Hellenic cruises. These cruises were known
by some as 'the Church of England at sea,' and while that is not true, it
caught something of the feel of the thing. There were lectures rather than
talks, and the passengers did homework instead of playing Bingo. There
was also what was called a 'clerical lecturer,' and this was me. It was rather
like being a college chaplain. You did not talk much about religion, but you
wandered around the ship, occasionally stopping to speak to people who
were thinking of jumping overboard after they had heard one lecture too
many.

I did talks on philosophy and the gods of the various countries we
were visiting. These were rather difficult to give, as religion is a notoriously
contentious topic, which is usually censored on cruises. Also, while most
people knew very little about these things, there were always one or two
world experts present who knew much more than I did about many things I
was talking about. However, one thing I have learned about being a professor is that if you say nothing, put your head in your hands, and an agonised
expression on your face, most people will accept that you are a very profound thinker. Perhaps they will think they have missed the point or said
something rather stupid. One can always hope.

As well as being extremely pleasant, the cruises gave first-hand experience of many different cultures, though quite often members of those
cultures behaved differently from the way they were supposed to. As is the
case with most academics, most of my knowledge came from books, and
I gave a very clear account of how Buddhists did not believe in a soul, or
continuing self. But when we visited a famous Buddhist monastery in Thai-
land, the head monk (who happened to be an ex-American marine) said,
"Where did you hear that rubbish?" He obviously had not read the same
books as me. But he was an abbot, and obviously a real living Buddhist. It
turned out that he just denied that there was a changeless element identical
with ultimate reality within everyone, but he was quite happy to say that

we continued to be the same people from one day to the next. Still, it was a salutary surprise.

Some other things were more difficult to deal with. I took great pains to explain that it would be a great insult to Hindus to call them idol-worshippers, but when we met a Hindu priest in Kerala, he said, "Come into my temple and see my idols," which rather took the wind out of my sails.

Again, we went to see a Jain temple in India, and I had explained that Jains did not believe in God, but our local guide insisted on showing us the statues of the gods in the temple (they were not gods, but liberated souls, but I admit they did look very like gods—and the guide turned out to be a Christian who did not know much about Jains).

The actual world is much more complicated than the one we read about in books. And one of the difficulties in understanding other cultures is that it is all too easy to translate what other people say in quite misleading ways. That is apt to give rise to quarrels that have little basis in reality. Real understanding takes a long time and a lot of initial sympathy, and even then we can never be sure we have got it right. The hardest and most important thing is never to describe a religion in terms that its adherents would not accept. This is much more difficult than it sounds, and is essential to true understanding in matters of belief.

SEEING THE WORLD

The faculty at King's had an exchange programme with universities in the Netherlands and Belgium, and I visited most of the universities there, even picking up an honorary doctorate from the Free University of Amsterdam. In fact, I soon found myself on the academic touring circus circuit. I toured New Zealand, Australia, South Africa, Canada, and the United States, as well as East Cheam and Basingstoke. I gave talks in Italy and France, where I got to know truly international groups of people, which broadened my outlook considerably. I also was invited to Japan and Turkey, but in both those cases I was invited by organisations that were, unknown to me, politically active and suspect, and I think they wanted a British academic to give the impression that they had Western academic respectability and approval. They obviously did not realise that I was not very respectable, and that I did not really approve of them (both organisations were extremely nationalistic, it turned out, and translated what I said into things I had never thought of). I was even made a member of a Japanese Shinto sect, though when they discovered how much (or how little) money I had, they stopped contacting me, and I never heard from them again.

It was considered important in academic life to have an international reputation, at least in the academic world. I had a good start, since I had already been in the University of Wales as well as Glasgow in Scotland and the very English Cambridge, so I considered that I was already known internationally. But I am not sure that counted.

One important thing that I learned was that language can be very important and very troublesome in religion. If you try to find an English translation of *nirvana* or *Tao* you are in big trouble. The English translation of the Hebrew of Ecclesiastes 11:1, in the Authorised Version, says, "cast thy bread upon the waters, for thou shalt find it after many days." That sounds suitably spiritual and refined. But the Good News Bible translates this as: "Invest your money in foreign trade, and one of these days you will make a profit." That translation is contested, but it shows how things can be interpreted in very different ways. Then again, there was the occasion when I said in a vote of thanks after a conference in Japan, "The English are perhaps well known for their understatement" (meaning to imply that when I said the conference was "quite good," I meant it was extremely good), and I was told that this came out in Japanese as "The English are well known for speaking in very short words." Translations can be extremely contentious and even misleading, as we do well to remember when reading the Bible in English. That fact also explains many of the historical differences between Eastern and Western Christians, and in general between Eastern and Western believers, who speak different languages. Huge and sometimes tragic differences can easily arise from simple linguistic misunderstandings. That does not mean we should stop trying to have such discussions. It does mean that we must be much more aware of the way words can generate misunderstandings and be more aware of the limitations of human languages.

THE WORLD CONGRESS OF FAITHS

Around this time, I also became the joint chair of the World Congress of Faiths and joint editor of *Religious Studies*, the main British religious studies journal. The World Congress of Faiths was an offshoot of the first-world Parliament of Religions, held in Chicago in 1893. The idea of the parliament was to increase mutual understanding between the various religions of the world. One major problem, straight away, was the large number of religions that refused to take part in it. Many thought that the very existence of the parliament was an attack on the obvious truth of their own religion. Some even thought that theirs was the only religion, and all the others were pseudo-religions or plain superstitions. However, the parliament did bring a remarkable group of religions to meet together, and at least it enabled them to eat together. Or it would have done, if various religious had not regarded as unclean and forbidden most of the foods that other religious folk were eating.

One of the most influential figures at the conference was an Indian thinker, Vivekananda, who travelled the USA telling groups of ladies that they were divine—which they rather liked, and had always suspected, though they had been told by their own Christian churches that they were miserable sinners. This was the beginning of the Californiarisation of a number of Indian and Eastern faiths. Various gurus and spiritual masters found that in America it was fairly easy to travel the country talking incessantly about the virtues of silent meditation, and becoming millionaires riding in luxurious cars by preaching the importance of renunciation. In fact, the versions of Eastern thought they proclaimed were mostly quite new to the East, and had been exported there by Westerners who had been brought up on Hegel and Schopenhauer. The words they used were all exotically Eastern, but they were re-interpreted to fit Western ideals of progress and self-realisation, whereas originally they had been more concerned with despair of worldly happiness and with self-renunciation.

I should make it clear that I do not disapprove of this—though it can be disconcerting to an outsider to find a spiritually exalted teacher riding around in a Rolls-Royce. It is rather an indication of the fact that religions are very susceptible to change and partial fusion with different streams of thought, even when they claim that their teachings have remained the same since before the Great Pyramids and are utterly unique.

One example of this can be found in Aldous Huxley's book, *The Perennial Philosophy* (1945), in which he claims that there is an ancient religious tradition that has remained unchanged throughout human history, and has always been known to those who have been initiated into its secrets. In fact, it is the *Advaita Vedanta* (non-dualist commentary on the Vedas and Upanishads) of Sankara, in sixth-century India, and is only one of twelve quite different interpretations of Indian scriptures. That interpretation has in turn been revised in recent years by an unacknowledged appeal to the work of some nineteenth-century European philosophers. All these things can be discovered by a little painstaking historical research.

Such research often, even usually, shows that the history of religions is in part a history of such changes, and of attempts to resist them. Such attempts, however, only succeed in producing yet another creative (or perhaps destructive) change, as doctrines that were at first radically innovative become the guardians of rigid and dogmatic traditions. In this way, the modern phenomenon of Christian fundamentalism appeals to the words of the New Testament as the essential foundation of faith, whereas in the earliest years of Christian faith there was not even any New Testament to appeal to, and most later Christian doctrines—like the incarnation or the nature of the Trinity or of the atonement—had not yet been developed. A radical interpretation of Jewish messianic thought was thereby turned into precisely the sort of conservative authoritarian appeal to final revealed truth that Christian faith had put in question by challenging the importance of obedience to the Torah (obedience to which is demanded by most of the Bible).

HOW RELIGIONS HAVE CHANGED

It was considerations of this sort that led me to think that it was of great importance to ask of any religious truth-claim: *By whom* was it first made? *Why* was it made? *In what context* did it originate? And what might be *a contemporary move of a similar sort,* in our very different cultural context? These thoughts did not make me less religious, or less concerned with knowledge of spiritual reality. But they did make me much more aware of the limitations of human language and understanding, and of the need constantly to rethink and expand the interpretations of spiritual reality that we inherit from our own cultural traditions.

In my own cultural context, it seemed to me that there were three main factors that called for relevant change. There was the rise of the natural sciences, which completely changed our worldview. There was the emergence of a more global awareness, as communication and travel made knowledge of other traditions more accessible, and ignorance of them more inexcusable, and indeed dangerous. And there were the great moral and political revolutions of the European Enlightenment, which generated a concern for social justice and for the equal freedom and responsibility of all in the organisation of society.

Religions, like all human institutions, include both people who wish to preserve old and loved traditions, and people who feel the need to adapt old beliefs in view of commitment to new knowledge and what they feel are more universal values. There is a delicate balance to be sought between these contrasting temperaments, and that balance is hard to find. In many ways, the biggest cultural battle of our time is not religion versus atheism. It is the defence of traditional values versus the claim to advance to new insights and more universal conceptions of value. In this battle different sorts of religion, indeed, different attitudes within each religion, take different sides. There is no formula for getting the balance right, but it is surely an advance in understanding to see that the past should not be forgotten, but that there is also a need to advance, and therefore to change, in knowledge and understanding.

CHRIST CHURCH, OXFORD 1991–2003

MY TIME AS A professor of the history and philosophy of religion was very important in developing my own faith. It was, however, ended by something that I had never expected or even thought of. One day I received a letter in a plain white envelope. Inside the envelope was another envelope with the royal coat of arms on it. Inside that envelope was a letter from the prime minister saying that the regius chair of divinity at Oxford University was vacant, and could he give my name to the Queen. I had not the slightest idea what this meant, but I was given a telephone number to ring if I had any questions. I had, so I rang the number. How many names is the PM giving to the Queen, I asked, and why? I was told that mine was the only name, and that if I accepted, she would appoint me to the chair. I was also told that if I did not accept, I was not to tell anyone—from which I inferred that a long list of people had quite possibly already turned the job down, and they had come to me as a last resort. But who was I to complain?

I also had reservations about being a professor of divinity. What, I asked, was divinity? Well, it is anything to do with the Bible or religion, I was told. Relying heavily on the word 'anything,' I reckoned that I might manage that. Just to check, I went to check with Rowan Williams, who was Lady Margaret Professor and at Christ Church, a large and prestigious college of which I would become a senior member, and said that since my main competence was in philosophy, I was not sure I should be a professor of theology. He assured me that it would be alright, because we could teach joint seminars; he would do the theology, and I would do any philosophical bits that were left over. Re-assured, I decided to accept the chair. But just a couple of years later, Rowan went off to be a bishop, and wound up as the archbishop of Canterbury. I considered this was a betrayal of trust, and all he left me with was his Welsh Bible. Just as I had become a moral philosopher by accident, so now I was becoming a theologian by accident—misled by the archbishop of Canterbury (though I accept that it was not really his fault).

When I was duly appointed, I received a letter from the Queen, which had to be read out in public, saying that she, of her "especial grace, certain knowledge, and mere motion," was appointing me to be the regius professor of divinity. I did think, however, that now I was going to be a professor of divinity, I ought at least to get a degree in theology. I thought I might as well start at the top, so I applied for a doctorate of divinity from Cambridge. This degree is awarded on the basis of published work, which has to be judged to be of international standard. Hoping that somebody might think that (you never find out who your examiners are, and there were some people I might have been rather worried about), I submitted some of my work, and fortunately I obtained the degree. In fact, I turn out now to have six university degrees, which does seem rather excessive, and may give the impression that I am badly in need of re-assurance. But it is really not my fault. It turns out that Oxford and Cambridge have (or maybe used to have) a practice known as incorporation. If you get a job at one of these universities, and have a degree from the other one, you get given the corresponding degree at your new university. Having an Oxford research degree, when I went to Cambridge I was given a Cambridge MA. Then I went back to Oxford, and so I got given an Oxford MA. In a similar way, when I got a Cambridge DD, and was at Oxford, I also got an Oxford DD. Thus, I did not actually spend all my time sitting exams to get more degrees. They just happened.

I also become a canon of Christ Church, which was especially attractive to me. This was because Christ Church was, uniquely in England, and perhaps in the world, indivisibly a college of Oxford University and an Anglican cathedral. Indeed, the tutors, who would in other colleges be called Fellows, were called Students, because in times long past they had been students of the canons, who really ran the place. That was no longer true, but this being Ye Olde England, the college went on pretending that it was true. The canons, six of them, even held the key to the college safe, in which was kept the college seal, without which no financial transactions could be made. Few of us knew in detail what the transactions were, and we were expected to open the safe when required, but the old tradition continued. It was, I imagine, rather like being the Queen.

Tom Quad, Christ Church

"THIS PRECINCT AND PECULIAR PLACE"

Christ Church is officially described as "a peculiar place" in medieval jargon, and it remains very peculiar in many ways. Most people do not know about the peculiar terminology Christ Church uses. Later, when I was buying something in a shop, the assistant asked me my job. I said I was a Student of Christ Church. She said she just had to ring her manager, and I heard her say, "This man says he is a student at some church," which obviously did not sound as if I was a good financial bet. But it was not being a Student that appealed to me. It was the thought of all the wonderful choral music, which is one of the great traditions of English cathedrals. As a canon, I would preach and take services in the cathedral, and the music in those services was without doubt one of the high spots in the English musical world. I found in music a disclosure of meaning and beauty that spoke to me of a reality transcending and transforming the everyday routines of human existence. To think that I could get paid for listening to that for the rest of my working life was irresistible. It was also a relief not to have to attend to the meaning of the words I sang too closely, since nobody has to believe what they sing, and religious people do sing some very peculiar words sometimes.

Some very odd expectations went with being a canon of Christ Church. A very senior member of the university said to me, "I hope you are not going to be like some of the other new canons of Christ Church. They have taken to hanging around after the services, trying to speak to people." Religion, he thought, was a very private affair, and conversation could only spoil it. Priests should do their job, and not pretend to be friendly to people they had often never met before, and would probably never meet again.

This was a problem at Christ Church. As a beautiful and famous cathedral, it attracted thousands of tourists every year. The cathedral was often full, but many members of a typical congregation had no idea of what was going on and did not speak English. I remember an occasion when I was taking Choral Evensong, trying to explain, as the service progressed, what was happening and why we did it. After the service, ignoring the advice of my learned colleague, I hung around afterwards and asked one person who was leaving whether my explanations had been helpful. She bowed graciously, and said, "I speaking no English, thank you." I never tried explaining Evensong again. For most of the congregation, it was obviously a complete waste of time.

Christ Church had been the home of Lewis Carrol, author of *Alice in Wonderland*, and a mathematician of some note. It used to be the case that most people visited the college because of that, but more recently some tourists have come to think of it as Harry Potter College. Visitors can buy broomsticks at the Porter's Lodge and play Quidditch in Christ Church meadows—a very tricky operation for old age pensioners. The dining hall was used in the Harry Potter movies, as the dining room of Hogwarts School, and the staircase had been made to move by computer magic. I was there when that part of the Harry Potter films was shot, and it was a very boring experience. The same scene was shot over and over again, and most of the time actors just stood around doing nothing. Our house was in Tom Quad, the main quadrangle, and I was asked not to come out of our front door, because they said I did not look academic enough, and also they would have had to pay me as an extra. My mother was very disappointed that I never appeared in the films.

Anyway, the college became a famous visitor attraction, not because of anybody who actually lived there, but because of a wholly fictional story about a place that never existed. Such is the modern world—and some people complain about religion being filled with fictitious elements. In the TV age, this ought to make religion more attractive than ever.

THE FACULTY OF THEOLOGY (AND RELIGION)

What I found pleasing, however, was that at last, whatever people might have thought, I was a genuine theologian. Not all my philosophical colleagues thought this was a good thing. At least one thought I had lost my intellectual faculties. Strangely enough, some of my new theological colleagues, upon whom I had been thrust by Her Majesty, thought that I was too philosophical by half. You just cannot please everyone. I also found that few theologians called themselves theologians. Some were Old Testament scholars, some New Testament scholars, some church historians, and some ancient linguists, but hardly anyone thought they were theologians.

What this shows is that there is something odd about the word 'theology.' The idea persists that a theologian has to defend the beliefs of some church or other. There are such theologians, of course. Catholic theologians who are licensed by the Vatican have to agree not to criticise the defined doctrines of their church. Anglicans, however, cannot agree on what their defined doctrines are, so that is not a big problem. In the old days, it was enough to believe anything defined before AD 451, after which date no further theological thought was presumed to have taken place, but the Protestant Reformation, the Roman Catholic Counter-Reformation, and the Thirty-Nine Articles of the Church of England threw some doubt on this. More recently it has all got much more vague, which suits me. I do not regard following Jesus as Lord as a matter of believing lots of propositions. For my part, I think actually believing that there is a God, and that Jesus came to be seen as manifesting God's nature and purpose, is definitely useful for a priest. But I would rather not be committed to saying in detail what this amounts to (well, I have said it in quite some detail in books I have written, but I do not insist that other people should read them). In any case, English universities are not any more, even if they once were, religious institutions, so theology—the study of beliefs and practices concerning God or spiritual reality—cannot be confined to any form of Christianity. Even Buddhists, I have found, who do not believe in a creator God, do not mind using the word 'theology'—thinking about *theos*—as long as the Greek '*theos*' refers to whatever is believed to be most real and valuable, whether it is personal or impersonal, describable or unsayable.

I devoted some time making this point in Oxford, and I am pleased to record that the faculty is now called the faculty of theology and religion, which clearly makes the point. At least I think it is clear, though discussions continue about just what theology and religion are. As far as I am concerned, this is a humanities discipline which seeks critical and discriminating understanding of some of the beliefs and practices which are of great importance to large parts of the world's population, and without knowledge of which some of the most vital questions about human existence would not be adequately pursued.

In accordance with these aims, I instituted a new degree (a Master of Studies) in the study of religion, and became the chairman of governors of a new institution, the Oxford Centre for Hindu Studies, as well as serving on the academic committee of the Islamic Centre, and supporting the institution of a Chair in Buddhist Studies. I did think, nevertheless, that I should try to make some contribution to Christian thought, and I thought I could best do this by relating such thought to modern science and to a more global understanding of religion. Not all my colleagues agreed. When I arrived, a rather conservative and long-time member of the faculty welcomed me, and said that the faculty were looking forward to new leadership and ideas. But when I told him what I had in mind, he said, "Oh, I did not mean that sort of thing." From that time on, he was firmly opposed to most of my new ideas. He even said on one occasion that I was destroying the Faculty of Theology single-handedly. Nevertheless, I respected his scholarship greatly, and always consulted him before I did anything new, knowing that this would tell me in advance what his best arguments against it were going to be.

MORE PECULIARITIES OF OXFORD

I have to admit that some of the practices of Oxford University are (at least, they were then) rather idiosyncratic. Soon after I arrived, I was asked if I would examine some of the theology papers for the final degree exams. I agreed, and said that I would like to ask the college tutors in theology what they had taught their students. One of my distinguished colleagues looked very shocked and said that this would be quite immoral. Tutors could discuss anything they wished with their students, but after all, he said, undergraduates came to Oxford to read theology, not to be taught it, and if I, the examiner, knew whatever it was that they had (perhaps accidentally) been taught, that would give them an unfair advantage in the exam.

I also discovered that attending lectures was optional, and that all the real work was done in one-to-one tutorials, in which sherry was served by all but the most ascetic of tutors. The consequence was that some lectures were given to almost empty rooms, and that a great deal of sherry was drunk. I never found out if lectures were given even in completely empty rooms, but I suspect they were, since lecturers were paid to give lectures, whether or not anyone was there.

I must add that the tutorial system is one of the glories of Oxford, that most students work very hard and successfully, and that things have changed a lot since I taught there. Yet when a group of tutors met to discuss what a memorable tutorial should be, the ones they remembered from their own Oxford education were the ones where the tutor was having a bath during the tutorial, or had absent-mindedly got a screwdriver stuck in his ear!

There are not so many eccentrics teaching at Oxford anymore, and I think it is rather a pity that we do not see lecturers turning up in their pyjamas or forgetting which direction they were walking in. One eminent professor during my time took all the completed examination scripts, posted them to himself, and then forgot what he had done with them. There was considerable panic in the faculty until the scripts arrived at his house a day or two later. Now, I believe, tutors have to fill in forms before each tutorial stating what their aims and objectives are. Since many of them refuse to see the difference between an aim and an objective, they find it difficult to get the tutorial started. They also have to write two peer-reviewed journal articles a year, fully referenced and footnoted, which results in journals being filled with useless but impeccably referenced articles on more and more obscure books that nobody has previously found, or even thought worth looking for, in the deepest recesses of the Bodleian Library.

Such demands might make sense in the natural sciences, where new research does produce new and useful results. But in the humanities, which are largely concerned with understanding and appreciating the intellectual and artistic endeavours of the past, it does not make sense to ask for new discoveries which contribute to economic success or new techniques of health care. Asking scholars in such subjects as theology to contribute to the economic well-being of the nation, is rather like asking a hedgehog to contribute more to the national milk supply. They (not the hedgehogs) contribute to the life and hopefully to the well-being of the mind, but they often contribute little to the Gross National Product of a nation.

THE BRITISH ACADEMY

It was at this time that I gave the Gifford lectures at the University of Glasgow, which were published as *Religion and Revelation* (1994). It turned out to be the first volume of a five-volume systematic theology (though most people think there are only four volumes, possibly because they do not want to read any more, but also because the last one has a different publisher). After all, that was the sort of thing theologians used to do in the old days, so I thought it was time I revived the custom. There were two elements that had not usually been included in such books. One was an informed enquiry into the views of religions like Islam, Hinduism, Buddhism, and Judaism. The other was an attempt to align religious belief with the findings of modern science. Because of this, I called it a 'comparative theology,' meaning that it did consider a number of religious traditions, without trying to establish the clear superiority of one of them, though it was obviously written by someone in a broadly Christian tradition. And it did compare religious and scientific beliefs, to see how they could be positively related.

I have to say that the series had little impact. I suspect most people thought I had taken on more than I could handle. I tried to avoid that charge by concentrating on particular writers from religious traditions whose works were translated into English. I was not really trying to compare religions as such, but to set the views of particular eminent religious individuals alongside each other. Anyway, the books passed quietly away, to rest in peace in the Bodleian Library, and wait for some future DPhil student who could not find a decent subject for research and might one day stumble across them.

All was not lost, however. For my efforts to increase understanding between religions, and to see how science impacted on religious belief, in 2000 I was elected to a fellowship of the British Academy, the premier association in Britain for those who are thought to have made major contributions to scholarship in the humanities. I later discovered that my main sponsor for this fellowship was John Macquarrie, whom I considered to be the foremost British theologian of the twentieth century, and who had also, like me, been at Glasgow University, and had been influenced by the Scottish tradition of philosophical idealism. I was naturally very pleased about this, though I have found that I am often thought to be a fellow of the Royal Academy, which is the premier society in Britain for very good artists. I have never painted anything since a schoolmaster sent one of my paintings in my art class to a psychiatrist for a diagnosis. Since then, I have never quite felt the same about art.

THE ROCKEFELLER FOUNDATION

At about this time, I was also offered a month's residence at the Rockefeller Foundation villa at Bellagio on Lake Como, a large and luxurious palace at which groups of selected scholars from various disciples could reside, on condition that they worked on a research project, and discussed things with each other. The staff, being American, had put up little notices about the place, like the one at the bottom of the very large garden, which ran down to the lake, saying, "Danger of water." That was, I suppose, to prevent people from suing the Foundation if they fell in the lake.

The residence was actually a great opportunity to undertake a personal research project, and to be able to discuss it with novelists, artists, scientists, and historians of some standing. It so happened that the group I was with consisted almost entirely of people who had little interest in religion. It was therefore a very challenging experience to encounter scholars who were very suspicious of anything called 'theology.' I spent the month trying to convince them that there really were serious questions about whether there was value and purpose in the universe, and that most of the great classical philosophers—people like Plato, Aristotle, Leibniz, Kant, Hegel, and many more—had thought there was. It was therefore impossible, I said, to claim knowledge of the history of human thought without gaining responsible, sympathetic yet critical, understanding of their arguments, which all involved claims that there was a spiritual dimension to human experience.

I think I convinced them of that, though they still did not like the word 'theology,' so I suggested that they used another word for critical, informed, and reflective thought about the place of value and purpose in human experience. Unfortunately, a month was not long enough to agree on another word, though, in the tradition of Plato, we drank a great deal in the attempt to find one. All this helped to convince me that there was a great deal of serious academic work to be done in exploring historical thinking about religious issues before what seems to me the modern prejudice that they are no longer of interest could be countered.

Anyway, at the end of my residence—which was, I must say, very productive and during which I learned as much from my fellow scholars as they did from me—my wife and I were driven from the palace in a large limousine. The driver asked where we would like to go, and we said, "Drop us at the nearest bus stop, please." That was a perfect instance of our scholarly existence as a mixture of caviar and relative poverty. We lived in luxury in a palace for a month, and then caught the bus home.

THE WORLD ECONOMIC FORUM

Thinking about caviar and poverty, I recall that during these years, I was also invited to participate in the World Economic Forum, in Davos, Switzerland. This was an annual meeting of the leading industrialists and politicians of the world—mostly of the Western capitalist world, it is true. I was intrigued to discover that the biggest and most luxurious hotel rooms were booked by the CEO of Coca Cola, which is a comment on the priorities of the Western world. The annual meetings, in which I took part for a few years, were often said to be good places for world leaders to meet in secret and exchange plans to rule the world. However, if there ever was a plot to globalise and control the world, I never heard even a whisper of it . . . in all the years I was there. Actually, the idea was to get influential opinion leaders to discuss issues of justice and global human welfare, and exchange differing perspectives on what the human future could be.

This is, I suppose, where people like me came in. We gave talks, hosted dinners, and led seminars on the main ethical issues of the day, and on how religions might work together to improve the human condition. I found these meetings with a very international group of people who had important roles in their societies very informative and sometimes inspiring.

Of course, it must be said that not everyone was primarily interested in such matters. I remember the CEO of one major industrial company saying to me, "I did not have time to come to your one-hour-long talk. Just tell me what you said in two sentences." I was relieved that I at least had two sentences, but I think some of the finer points of my talk might have been missed. There have been criticisms of Davos as a cosy club for the capitalist elite. Nevertheless, it always seemed to me that it was wholly good that an international meeting of world leaders did convene to discuss the latest scientific discoveries, the main political problems of the world, and ethical priorities for the future of humanity.

Davos introduced me to the world of big business, and enabled me to see how complex its problems were. Its main impact on me was to convince me that unrestrained capitalism was liable to lead to gross inequality and injustice. Yet complete state control of business undermines creative initiative and responsibility. The decisive factor is to encourage among leaders of industry the development of concern for the common good of all humanity, and especially for those who are poor and disadvantaged through no fault of their own. There are no easy answers, but there is little hope for the world if the desire for personal profit outweighs a commitment to attempt to ensure the well-being of all people. For all its faults, religious faith is one of the major factors that may be able to inculcate such a moral sense.

THE TEMPLETON FOUNDATION

Similar considerations led me in the direction of the Templeton Foundation. Sir John Templeton was an American-born investment counsellor and philanthropist, who made a great deal of money by inspired and contrarian investing, and he generously decided to give a large amount to the search for increased understanding in and of religion. Since this was exactly what I had devoted my academic life to doing, I strongly approved of the Foundation's aims, and when I was asked to become an advisor to the Foundation I gladly agreed.

I was very surprised to find that the Foundation was apparently very controversial, though I should have been used to the idea that people have extremely strong feelings about religion, whether they are for or against it. I have been told by one rather extreme secularist that I should be put in prison because I hold religious beliefs, and I have also been told by an equally extreme Christian that I will fry in hell forever because I hold the wrong religious beliefs. It seems that many people, whether they are religious or not, just love to dominate other people. The religious are persecuted by dictators and tyrants who hate religion (and there are plenty of those in the world) and the irreligious are persecuted by the same sort of dictators and tyrants if those dictators happen to be religious (or say they are).

I have not found that Templeton persecutes or even threatens anyone, so why should anyone hate it except for the fact that its founder generally approved of (some kinds of) religion? It is true that Sir John had one or two personal beliefs that I did not share. He thought that it was possible to learn 100% more about God in a short time, and that one could make progress of a scientific sort in religion. I was sceptical of these beliefs, and privately hoped that some people would learn 100% less about God than they claimed to know, and stop thinking that they could find some sort of scientific evidence for such things as the existence of Noah's ark and the date of the end of the world. It turned out that Sir John was also a great believer in contrarian thinking, and liked the fact that I disagreed with him. Not that he ever followed any of my advice.

One positive thing that he did was to finance conferences of leading scientists, religious and non-religious, together with some academic philosophers and theologians, to explore questions like whether or not there was purpose and value in the universe. These conferences were in exotic and luxurious places—they had to be to get eminent scientists to go to them—but their great value was that some of the best minds in the world, both religious believers and atheists, met and discussed some of the great questions of the world, in a convivial and totally free environment.

No attempt was ever made to get everyone to agree, much less to adopt some religion. Atheists have received the Templeton Prize, awarded annually for outstanding thought about religion, and the Foundation is committed to no religious beliefs. So why do people complain about it? It can only be out of an intolerance of religion so deep that even informed discussion of it ought to be banned.

PUBLIC DEBATES

For my Oxford colleague Professor Richard Dawkins, whom I know well and respect for his scientific work, there can be no informed discussion of religion. Theology as a subject simply does not exist, except in the sense that astrology or alchemy exist. Since it does not exist, he has never read any theology, which makes me wonder how he knows it is so bad. I myself have found that it is at least as difficult and sophisticated as philosophy, though I suspect he does not think that exists either.

I have had public debates with Professor Dawkins and with Peter Atkins, an even more vehement Oxford enemy of religion. I easily won these debates, but there is a reason for that. In Oxford debates, as in the British House of Parliament, you do not have to listen to the arguments before you vote. You can sit in the bar while the debate is in progress then come into the debating chamber just before the vote, cast your vote, and go home. The Oxford Christian Union organised lots of people to do just that and vote for me, whatever I had said. Winning was not such a big deal.

During the debates, no holds were barred. Peter Atkins claimed that my religious beliefs were the result either of too much oxygen in the brain or too little, I forget which. He did not admit that his beliefs were due to chemical brain-processes too, and so they were presumably just as specious as mine. Dawkins asserted that I was suffering from a delusion, but it was hard to see how he could prove this without giving me a full psychiatric examination. He asserted that I could not prove God existed, and was un-impressed to hear that Professor Ayer, David Hume, and I could not even prove that Richard Dawkins existed. In real life, strict proof is very rarely required. It is more a matter of what makes the best sense of one's experi-ence. There are arguments about key cases (like values, numbers, motives, and purposes), but it is not reasonable to assume that if an opponent differs from oneself, they are mentally ill. That sounds like abuse, not argument. Maybe it is even a delusion.

BOOKS AND IDEAS

During this time, as well as my 'Religion and . . .' series, I wrote *God, Chance, and Necessity* (1996), a study of the role of the interplay of chance and necessity in the natural world; *God, Faith, and the New Millennium* (1998), purporting to propound a religious faith fit for the twenty-first cen-tury; and *God: A Guide for the Perplexed* (2002), which did not promise to leave people less perplexed about God, but on the contrary, argued that perplexity was no bad thing when tackling ultimate questions on the edge of human understanding.

Roughly speaking, my attitude is that materialism is an unduly dog-matic and poorly evidenced philosophical theory that has only been held by a small number of well-known philosophers. Modern science has made amazing new discoveries about the nature of the physical universe, and it is discovering new things every year. At its best, it is creative and in many respects provisional, and it does not deal with aspects of reality that are not physical, if there are any—so as science it can neither confirm or deny them. As for the immense diversity of religions, it just is the case that humans will disagree about almost anything, given the chance, and all religions are influenced by their histories and their basic value-judgments. Yet there is a widely accepted basic core of belief that there is a spiritual reality from which humans seem to be estranged, and there is a way of achieving a more positive relationship to it.

All this seems pretty obvious to me, but there is no doubt that many people disagree. Since my views predict widespread disagreement, this is no surprise. The only way forward seems to be to accept the cultural limitations of our own views, but do the best we can to make them consistent with the best established facts and values we know about. This is not the sort of certainty many would like. But I am certain it is true—or perhaps, given what I have just said, I should not be certain, but just say that it is my firmly held belief.

Since my views depend so much on gaining accurate knowledge of other cultures and values, I have travelled widely to many parts of the world, seeking to meet people of differing cultures and values. However, linguistic difficulties often arise, which is why I have travelled more in the United States than anywhere else. There they speak a language closely similar to English (if this sounds patronising, the same can be said about parts of the UK, including the part I come from). And there are many differing cultures and values in the USA. I think it is fair to say that almost any religion in the world can be found there, even though even the most ascetic faiths have to co-exist with cheeseburgers and fries. I have visited and lectured in many American universities, some famous and some unpretentious yet delightful, and was even invited to teach for semesters at Tulsa, Claremont, and Chapman Universities.

EVOLUTION AND OTHER STORIES

There was one American university, however, which shall remain nameless, that invited me for a semester. It was a Christian university of a certain sort, and one of the trustees wrote to me and said, "Professor Ward, we will be honoured to have you here. But I have looked at your website, on which you say you are a liberal. In view of that, we think it would be better if you did not speak to anyone while you were here." Accordingly, I went during the summer vacation and enjoyed a quiet holiday on a deserted campus. Actually, the academic staff did speak to me, and we had a discussion about evolution, but it had to be held behind locked doors, in case one of the trustees came in.

I don't know why evolution is such a big issue in some places, since we all evolve in the womb from an egg, but I have never heard anyone argue that this means we are descended from an egg, and so can readily be fried or boiled. Does it matter where we started from, if we are now rational moral agents? Anyway, most of us are neither fully rational nor moral, so it is a very odd argument that we should be treated as we were once or even as we actually are now, instead of looking ahead to see what we can become. Speaking personally, I am very happy to have been a fertilized egg, if it is possible for me to become more like an angel. In fact, that would make life a rather interesting challenge, and I am surprised that so many Americans, who tend to think that everything is getting better, fail to see that the implication is that things must once have been much worse. That is, there has been a sort of evolution. The truth is that we are always evolving.

Anyway, that university was the exception. It was very different at Claremont University (then, Claremont Graduate School), near Los Angeles. I stood in for the philosopher John Hick for a semester, and was able to undermine all his favourite theories before he returned. I am sure that he was able to re-instate them—in fact, I think he was the best, or at least one of the best, philosophers of religion of the twentieth century, and we agreed with each other about the most important issues. He was well able to stand up to some impertinent criticism from me.

I loved teaching in the US. In Britain, you can walk into a class and say, "I have just refuted the general theory of relativity," and they will say, "Oh yes, we have heard that one before." But in America, you walk in and say, "The sun is shining today," and they will reply, "Gee, that is amazing. And it's really true. Thanks for the news, Coach." The American experience is so much more encouraging.

The only trouble with having an English accent is that in Hollywood films if any male speaks with an English accent, you know he is the villain. I am not sure why that is, but I suspect it goes right back to the American Revolution—sorry, the War of Independence.

The most remarkable thing about the US is the immense range of thought that flourishes there. Everyone and anyone can start their own religion, and they do. There are religions that believe we are ruled by a secret society of lizards from another galaxy, there are religions that believe the Messiah is living in New York, and there are religions that believe all religions are true, despite the fact that nearly all those religions disagree with them. In one town I visited, there was an Apostolic Church, and a True Apostolic Church. I was disappointed to find that there was not a Really True and Really Primitive Apostolic Church—though there was a sign by the roadside that said, "Antiques made daily," and that may well have been it.

Quite a number of such churches believed themselves to have the only reliable interpretation of the Bible, and it did make me wonder how clear the Bible really was if people could differ so much about what it said. They mostly said that the Bible was self-interpreting. When they held Bible study groups, someone would read out a passage of the Bible and say, "My interpretation of this passage is that it means what it says," and everyone else would say "Amen," and that was that. It seems rather obvious that the Bible does mean what it says, but that people do not really know what that is. It may as well have been written in Hebrew and Greek for all they know. On second thoughts, it was. But maybe the Holy Spirit tells them what it means even if they do not read Hebrew or Greek. Maybe.

John Hick, incidentally, was banned from ministering to Presbyterian churches in California when he was teaching there, because he did not believe the right things. Back in England, he remained acceptable, possibly because English Presbyterians are open to a number of differing interpretations of the faith. I think this is a definite improvement.

I strongly approve of freedom of speech and opinion, but it clearly has its dangers, which the internet has made apparent. The problem concerns whom one can trust. It seems to me that one should not be content with information provided by only one source, however reputable. One should beware of defamatory language about opinions other than one's own, especially if one knows little about them. And one should take note of the reputation of a source among those who are well trained and experienced in the relevant subject.

This means that in matters of religion one should attend to traditions other than one's own. One should disregard those who seem to mock or deride other traditions. And one should seek out reputable scholars when thinking about subjects like biology or the history of religions, though one should never think that they are infallible.

This will not eliminate disagreements, but at least disagreements will be generally respectful of other views, and able to provide a rational defence of one's own. The obvious exception is where views cause obvious and detectable harm to the well-being of others. Even then, care should be taken to seek the least harmful outcome to any situation.

Following these guidelines should eliminate adherence to those I have seen who carry signs saying things like "God hates fags," or who reject evolution without being competent in biology. But it will leave plenty of silly or fantastical views to choose between. I suppose that, looking at it as objectively as possible, mine may seem to be one of them. But that just means that it would not fit into some other quite widespread frameworks for interpreting human experience of the world. And that, after all, is true of all of us.

CLAREMONT AND PROCESS THOUGHT

It was at Claremont that I came into contact with the Center for Process Studies. Although process philosophy was invented by A. N. Whitehead, an Englishman, nobody in England seems to have heard of it, though it is quite well established in the USA. One reason for this may be that Whitehead invented a technical vocabulary that is almost impossible to understand, and few people have managed to read to the end of his main work, *Process and Reality* (1929).

The part of his system that most interested me was his bold revision of the idea of God. Instead of thinking of God as a timeless, changeless, simple reality, omnipotent and omniscient—which is more or less the traditional Christian view—he proposed that God had a threefold nature, which he called the primordial nature, the consequential nature, and the superjective nature (this is a good example of the difficult technical terms he used).

The primordial nature of God was a realm of possibilities, rather like Plato's world of 'Forms.' We could say that God thinks of all possible worlds. These are possibilities, not actualities, so there is lots of potentiality in God. This rejects one traditional view of God as 'pure actuality,' which can be found in Thomas Aquinas, for example. God has a lot of potential.

This might sound as if God has not yet reached maturity. That does not sound too good. However, all it really means is that there are infinitely many things that God could do, but has not done, and God would never come to the end of the divine creative possibilities.

If God is pure actuality, as Aquinas said, there are no merely possible things in God. So it is not possible for God to do or be anything other than what God does or is. This has always struck me as a marked limitation on the power of God. If you ask God to do anything really new, God has to say, "Sorry, that is not possible. I am what I am, and it is not possible for me to do anything else." Surely God would be more powerful if God could do lots of things that God does not actually do—like create a different universe.

Physicists talk a lot about possible worlds, and many of them think there really are many possible worlds, though they rarely pursue the question of where they are supposed to exist, if they are only possible. Some take the extreme view that all possible worlds actually exist, though there is still a problem about where they are. Being other spacetimes, they are obviously not in our spacetime. So they are literally nowhere, in no spatial or temporal relation to us. That gets rid of one form of materialism—the view that everything that can exist must be somewhere in our spacetime—straight away. Many physicists think there are lots of things that exist nowhere. They cannot have any reason to complain that God exists nowhere, since they already accept that lots of things, even whole universes, exist nowhere.

God may exist in the same nowhere as all those other universes. Some physicists call this superspace. But they are just making that up. There is no such place. It strikes me that it is much simpler and more elegant to say that all possible universes exist in the mind of God—for possible things can exist in minds, as far as we can see. The mind of God is nowhere, not in any space at all, and physicists of all people should have no problem with that.

POSSIBLE WORLDS AND VALUES—MY VIEW

While we are on the subject of possible worlds, there is another odd thing that physicists tend to say. When they think about possible worlds, they neglect to mention the most obvious things about them. They talk about such things as gravity and mass/energy and wave-functions. But they never talk about whether such worlds are good or bad. Questions of value do not enter into physics, yet they are the most important questions to ask about possible worlds. Are they good or bad?

Some possible worlds seem to be so horrible that they really should not exist—worlds where all sentient creatures are in terrible pain for ever, for instance. They may be mathematically possible, but they are not morally possible; they are too bad to exist.

The fact is that values are part of ontology. That is, if you make a list of the sorts of things that exist, values and disvalues, good and bad states, have to be on that list. Leibniz thought that a God would have to create the best possible world, and was satirised by Voltaire for this belief in his novel *Candide* (1759), where the hero, Pangloss, suffered innumerable disasters, but kept saying, "All is for the best in the best of all possible worlds."

Actually, Leibniz's view was more subtle than that, but the fact is that we can imagine many better, more pleasant, worlds than this. So why would a God create *this* one? It seems that, either God has to create this world, there is no alternative, or there are many sorts of worlds that are good in different ways, and God can create any of them, as long as the specific values of the world are obtainable in no other way, and the good overwhelmingly outweighs the bad things of that world.

There is good scientific evidence for the claim that we carbon-based life-forms could only exist in a universe with the physical laws and constants that actually obtain, which inevitably produce destruction and chance as well as creation and order. Human beings emerge in the course of cosmic evolution, and then produce values of a distinctive sort. It is plausible to think that the distinctive and otherwise unobtainable values of this world lie in what might be called the emergent self-realisation of communities of persons.

That might sound like my own invention of a difficult technical vocabulary. But what it means is that from a primal point of infinite energy and mass without structure, diversity, awareness, or conscious purposes (the Big Bang), the cosmos expands, cools, and diversifies into quarks, electrons, atoms, cells, nervous systems, and brains, to its present state on this planet of societies of conscious, valuing, and purposive persons—that is emergence. The potentialities of this world gradually unfold through processes of creative effort and striving by the parts of the universe itself—that is self-realisation.

GOD AS THE INFLUENCING IDEAL

There is a place for God in this scheme. Though what happens is due to the unfolding possibilities of the universe itself, God is the being that provides possible routes from initial unconscious simplicity to conscious organised complexity. The routes that are actually taken depend on the choices made by parts of the cosmos itself—though for billions of years these 'choices' are more like explorative fumbling than like fully conscious goal-directed actions. Nevertheless, the process has a direction and a goal, which is built into the system as a whole.

Whitehead calls this tendency in the universe towards understanding, beauty, and goodness, the superjective aspect of the divine mind. It could also be called the relational aspect, which generates and then actively responds to what happens in the cosmos. It is a sort of influence of ideal values on the way things in the universe go. It is as though the ideals attract things towards them, something that Aristotle had proposed, but it is an attraction that can be resisted or responded to in various ways.

This idea of a divine influence and power for goodness differs from some more traditional ideas of God as the all-determiner of the creation. Some Christians have thought that when God created the universe, God had already determined everything that was going to happen. If that was true, God could never change the divine mind, and could never respond in new ways to what happened, because God had already made it happen. But if God can create individuals that decide their own future, then God can co-operate with them to encourage positive, creative tendencies and frustrate negative, destructive ones. For many traditional views, people are like characters in a computer game. They do just what they are made to do. Whereas individuals might actually be creatively free, and make decisions that are really their own. I would rather be like this, even if it means that I would probably suffer and make some mistakes along the way.

GOD AS FELLOW-SUFFERER

Whitehead also speaks of a third, consequential, aspect of God. All the experiences of cosmic creatures and all the events of the cosmos are taken up, included, and integrated into the divine consciousness. This means that God feels what creatures feel, and is affected and changed by all that happens in the cosmos. He is, in Whitehead's words, "the fellow-sufferer who understands." God remembers perfectly all that has ever happened in the universe. In other words, the past is not completely lost. It exists in God.

If in this world goodness is overwhelmingly to outweigh evil, there must be some way in which creatures attain some sort of fulfilment. This involves the idea of immortality, since the final destination in this world is death. If you think that minds are not always limited to being in one body, this does not seem too difficult. After all, the bodies we have as children are very different from the bodies we have as old people. These bodies are admittedly closely connected in time, but I cannot see why there could not be a temporal gap, and then an instantaneous jump from infancy to old age. It would be rather surprising at first, but we could get used to it. It often happens in films, after all, and if Hollywood can do it, surely God can.

Whitehead himself was not committed to belief in immortality. But if God knows and remembers all that has ever happened, then it would be quite possible for dead people in new bodies to access all these events in the divine mind, to meet each other and lots of strange extra-terrestrial beings they had never seen before, and to continue their journeys towards the ultimate goal of complete understanding and bliss. That might be a sort of fourth aspect of God, which John MacQuarrie called the unitive aspect, in which all things would consciously share in the divine nature, and the divine nature would be fully expressed in a communion of love.

That may all sound hopelessly optimistic, but something very like it has to be true if this world is created by a God who knows, feels, and acts for a good reason. That reason, on this view, is to create new and distinctive values, and to share in their creation and appreciation with many finite minds.

It may be pushing things a little, but I think Christians can find in this idea a sort of Trinity: God is the Originator of all; the Spirit which responds to and works in the world to bring order out of chaos; and the eternal Word or Wisdom, which both enters into the world of suffering, and ultimately takes the world into the divine life. This is a more gender-neutral way of speaking of the Father, the Spirit, and the Son. These are all aspects of one cosmic mind which thinks, feels, and wills, which creates and relates dynamically to an emergent and self-realising creation.

This may be a rather presumptuous elaboration of parts of Whitehead's complex system, but it is a view of God that has certainly been influenced by process thought, and that helped me to develop my own theology.

RELIGION IN THE HEARTLAND OF AMERICA

I taught for a semester at Tulsa, Oklahoma, which took me to the heartland of America. Many people know about Tulsa only that, according to a well-known song, it takes twenty-four hours to get there. Now that we can fly, it doesn't take that long, but it is certainly a long way from Tulsa to the sea. For a Brit, that can be psychologically disturbing, and the nearest thing you can get to waves is the blue-grass prairie, which waves in the wind for as far as you can see.

Tulsa is a pretty city, with some Lloyd-Wright buildings of note and a couple of really fine museums. It also has a zoo, which my wife and I used to visit on 'polar bear' days, when admission was cheap because all the animals were freezing (insofar as it ever freezes in Tulsa), and we decided it would be only fair to join them. Tulsa was the home of Phillips Oil, and was once one of the richest cities in the world. Even when we went, many homes had oil derricks (or 'nodding donkeys,' as I think they were called) in their yards, which were great sources of energy supplies.

The university was well endowed and very well run. It should not be confused with the Oral Roberts University in Tulsa, where Ned Flanders, of *The Simpsons* fame, was educated. That is a bastion of fundamentalist Christian faith, and disappointingly I was never invited there. At one time they required that all the faculty of the medical school had to be able to speak in tongues. The consequence of that was that they had no medical school—though there was a group of people who wandered around the corridors giving diagnoses that nobody could understand—actually, not so unusual in medical schools.

There were some fundamentalists who came to my lectures at Tulsa University, and I managed to modify their views in some ways. The sort of modification I mean is manifested by the student who, at the end of the semester, said, "Dr. Ward, you have really opened my eyes. I now see that the six days of creation were not necessarily twenty-four hours long. They might have been longer." I hope that radical thought did not damage his faith too much.

I think it is true to say that Tulsa University was pretty conservative (so, of course, is Oxford), but the students were wonderfully open to new ideas, and eager to learn from this foreign person who spoke with such a strange accent. I confess that I took to saying things like, "He is a jolly good chap," because the students would say, "Please say that again," as it was just what they expected a Brit to say—even though at home I would never use such phrases.

I had gone to Tulsa at the invitation of a trust that sponsored Anglican academics, even though the university was technically Presbyterian, I think. The experience was a very rewarding one, partly because it showed how even people who share the same language and general belief-system can develop very different cultures or forms of life. In human life, there is always the danger of a breakdown of communication between different value-choices—which is increasingly apparent in the USA today—and it is universities like Tulsa that can help to build the understanding and tolerance that is necessary to the peaceful continuance of a free society.

MIDWEST EXPERIENCES

I don't know quite what I expected in Tulsa, but when I turned on my radio on my first morning there, I was amazed to hear the presenter says, "Tulsa University is now in the top ten among all American Universities, and I want to congratulate all those who put in so much hard work to makes this possible." I was impressed. "Yes, our football team has really outdone all expectations this year, and it is important to support them." That was more like it. Tulsa did indeed have a very good American football team. Sport was really important in the university, and many of my students were majoring in sports science, and doing my course as a sort of side-line. At the end of the semester, some students came to me in tears, saying that they had to get an A grade to continue their courses, and they had been to all my lectures and had listened very hard. I had to explain that they should really have written something as well. (I should add that I had some really good students too.)

We used to fly to Albuquerque at weekends, mostly to visit the American Indian mesas in New Mexico. My wife was an admirer of the American writer Tony Hillerman, who wrote crime novels set in Native American reservations. I was also very interested to find out about the rituals and traditions that the European colonisers had tried to wipe out, but that were experiencing something of a revival, with the more gruesome bits cut out. They showed the highly symbolic nature of religious language and ritual, dealing with real spiritual realities, but not in a literal way. I believe that the more logically articulated and often over-precise dogmatic features of much Western Christian religion need to be balanced by the more imaginative and narrative traditions of the world's indigenous peoples. In fact, the American Indian museum in Washington, with its exhibition of tribal creation stories, is the best introduction to understanding the creation story in Genesis that I have come across. It could be a good lesson for some Christians, especially at Oral Roberts University.

We also visited Arkansas, and we saw something of the other side of America. There were tumbledown shacks by the side of the road, surrounded by stacks of long-abandoned cars and various pieces of rusting farm equipment. This was not the America of roads paved with gold and opportunities for all. It was a heritage of the Great Depression, and it was clear that 'the land of opportunity' was also, for some, 'the land of shattered dreams' and for many others, 'the land of inescapable rural poverty.'

Feeling in need of a drink, we went into a local store and asked where we could get a bottle of wine. "That would be about twenty miles down the road in the next State," was the reply; prohibition was still a lived reality in some parts. We travelled twenty miles until we got to the state border. There was a small wooden shack and a man with a rifle. We crossed the border, bought our bottles of wine, carefully wrapped them in brown paper, and returned to our motel, where we surreptitiously consumed our illegal substances.

Guns were much in evidence in Arkansas. The car we rented had a bumper sticker that read: "I'm arming up for Armageddon," which we found vaguely embarrassing. And when we went to a restaurant, six men in cowboy hats and boots came in, sat down, took out their pistols, laid them on the table, joined hands, and prayed. We saw a side to religion we had not previously experienced. But we discovered that even some of the clergy had guns secreted in their clerical vestments during services, in case someone came in to shoot a few worshippers. We even came across groups that campaigned for their children to take guns to school, to defend themselves adequately. I could not think of anything more likely to increase the number of deaths by shooting, but at least they did not seem to be asking for their kids to take armoured tanks into school (though the vehicles they went to school in did look a bit like armoured tanks to us). We had hired a Mini Cooper, which was in constant danger of being squashed flat on the freeway by gargantuan SUVs. However, they sometimes found the car to be 'very cute,' and some vowed to buy one for their children to play with.

That was not our only adventure with wine. In Utah, we ordered two glasses each of Bordeaux, but were sternly told that the state only allowed one glass per person at a time to be on the table. However, as long as we drank each glass completely, and removed it from the table, we could then order as many as we liked, one at a time, of course. I am not sure that was completely in the spirit of the law, but it worked for us.

FREEDOM AND LIBERALISM

What we found hard to get used to was that half the people were extraordinarily kind and helpful, even stopping their cars to let us cross the road, which is unheard of in Britain. But the other half seemed to go around shooting people, drinking out of brown paper bags, and picking fights with strangers, especially strangers of different colours, in the street. America, they proclaimed, was the country of the free, but liberals were unpatriotic losers. I had always thought that liberals were by definition people who love freedom, and that America was one of the great liberal countries, but maybe freedom meant something different in parts of America—perhaps it meant, do what you want and take no notice of anyone else. The really odd thing is that even people in shacks in Arkansas were often opposed to liberals and Democrats. It seemed to be the triumph of advertising sponsored by the rich over the reality of poverty.

There is not much point believing that freedom is a great value, and then denying it to half the population. If freedom just means being left alone, that leaves the ill and the poor being left to die. I do not think any morally serious person could accept that. If it means being able to express your own personal talents and abilities, then there must be some way of organising things so that as many people as possible have the means to do so. There can be no freedom without social organisation, but it should be a form of organisation that can be held responsible for maximising freedom for all. It is hard to arrange such a social system, but it looks as if neither communism (or its apparently necessary preliminary form, the dictatorship of the workers) nor unrestrained capitalism (which becomes in effect the rule of the rich and successful) are likely to do it. Can America find the answer? I suspect that without a commitment to the moral values of justice, compassion, freedom, and trust—that is, without respect and care for every person without exception—no society can.

You might think that Christianity should provide the answer. But many versions of Christianity actually promote hatred of others, distrust of science, and rejection of cultural diversity. So that is not the answer. That sounds depressing. But what is needed is not just any kind of Christianity, but a scientifically informed, morally sensitive, and tolerant Christianity. Christians, and all people who believe and hope in a higher power for good, must commit their lives to the pursuit of the good for its own sake, and to the pursuit of social structures that support that pursuit, without thinking they have the final answers, and without expecting success or a resolution of all the world's problems. That, at least, is possible in the USA. Those who follow the example of Jesus know that the pursuit of the good is unrelentingly demanding and often seemingly futile. But small things can be accomplished. And people of the Spirit know that, while they hope for good in the world, this world is not their only hope.

CHAPMAN UNIVERSITY

We saw another side of America at Chapman University, in Orange County, one of the wealthiest of Californian enclaves. Chapman was a small but distinguished university, where there was a very lively religious studies department, headed by Nancy Martin, whose major interest was in devotional Hinduism, especially in Rajasthan. There were also some major theoreticians in quantum physics, and, strange as it may seem, there was a happy and positive relationship between these disciplines. After I gave a public lecture, arguing that the physical universe was the expression of mathematical information held in a cosmic mind, one physicist, Menas Kafatos, give me a copy of one the physics books he had written, (*The Non-Local Universe* [2001]) inscribed with the message, "To Keith, with my best regards for our common view." I was delighted to have this support from a scientist at the forefront of modern research.

Another public lecture I gave at Chapman was a debate about religious belief with the editor of *The Sceptic* magazine, the self-styled king of unbelievers. I was intrigued by the fact that I was given an armed guard, ostentatiously carrying a large revolver, and surprised that I, and not the sceptic, was the one who was thought to need such a guard. Apparently, religion is a serious matter in the USA—very unlike the UK, where nobody seems to worry very much about it. Anyway, I argued that I was sceptical about scepticism, and was sure that even sceptics seemed pretty sure that scepticism was correct. So it is OK to be sure in practice, if uncertain in theory, of some things of great moral importance, and that might include some religious things. I do not know if that convinced anybody, but at least I did not get shot, and fortunately my armed guard said that he agreed with me.

MORE AMERICAN ADVENTURES

While living in Orange, we used to listen to the firework display that concluded each day at nearby Disneyland. I could not resist visiting Disneyland, which said that it was "the happiest place on earth." If you had enough money, it was certainly happy in a way. But as I walked around the back of one of the amusement rides (for which there was, as usual, a mile-long queue, cleverly concealed by hiding the final half-mile in a large tent), I came across Mickey Mouse and Goofy having a conversation. Mickey was saying, "If I do just three more days' overtime, I will have enough money to pay my psychiatrist." And I wondered just how happy the place could really be.

On the other hand, when we visited Yosemite, I had a glimpse of real happiness. One of the great features of the USA is the institution of National

Parks, and the legally enforced (more social restrictions?) preservation of true wilderness shows a great concern to care for the wonders of the natural beauty of the world. It is hard to maintain that concern and to cope with the influx of tourists, which increases year by year. These days there is even a queue to get to climb Half Dome, and there are certainly queues in the peak season to find quiet spots for the contemplation of nature at Yosemite. It is still possible, however, if you walk more than a mile from a car park or fastfood outlet, to find a space to sit down.

It is probably not a good idea to look up websites which say things like, "The most beautiful view is from Happy Valley" or "Guide to secret gardens of delight." You may be sure that millions of others will have done the same thing, and the places will be crowded. You have to look for places that are really ugly and unpopular, and then you have a chance of being alone.

Sometimes, on our outings, we took things too far. Visiting the Living Desert outdoor museum, we rebelled against the tarmac paths on which we were supposed to walk, and the little notices that said, "Look right now for a great view" or "Leave this path at your peril," and decided to have a real desert experience. We left the path and set off up a smally stony creek. At last, it really was uncrowded. There was no one else there, and it was wonderfully quiet and peaceful. Except for a rattling sound coming from under some rocks. We looked down and saw that the rattle was coming from the back end of a snake. Looking more closely around, we saw rattlesnakes under almost every rock, all looking back at us, it seemed rather eagerly. I have to say that we descended from the creek faster than we had gone up it, and did not leave the tarmac paths again that day. When we got back to the main building, a guide said, "Rattlesnakes are really quite friendly, and will not usually attack you." This was meant to be reassuring, but we were a little bit unhappy that she only said what was 'usual,' and were only too aware that unusual things happen. Luckily, they did not happen to us that day.

Nature is beautiful, but it is also dangerous. California has great beaches, mountains, and forests. But in recent years it has suffered enormous forest fires, and of course there is always the danger of the San Andreas fault casting large parts of California into the sea. We did experience some small earthquakes, and they were quite big enough for us. There are also problems about the energy and water supplies, so while most lawns in Orange County were excessively green, we gathered that the amount of energy used to accomplish this was excessively large. I don't think this is a cause for despair, but it does mean that constant vigilance and effort is needed to ensure that the natural world is preserved and enhanced to become a safe and beautiful environment for life. Perhaps it means that human lives should become simpler and more restrained. Even in Orange County, my conversations with a new generation of young students makes me pretty confident that this is possible.

GRESHAM COLLEGE,
LONDON, 2004–2008

AFTER TWELVE HAPPY YEARS at Christ Church, during which I had no difficulty in sharing ministry with other canons who had very different views from mine on all sorts of subjects, ranging from the nature of Christ's incarnation to the possibility of keeping dogs (which were officially banned) by calling them cats (which no one had thought of banning) in college rooms, I reached the official retiring age. I was made an Emeritus Student of Christ Church, which enables me to turn up and annoy everyone in college whenever I feel like it. We moved to a house in Cumnor, a village near and virtually part of Oxford, and there I was a sort of unofficial curate at Cumnor Parish Church. But that was not the end of my university teaching career. I was invited to apply for the chair of divinity of Gresham College, in London. This was not a permanent post. It was held for three or four years, though I did two stints, due to one designated professor having a heart attack. It was a sort of high-level adult education programme, requiring about six lectures a year in the City of London. Gresham was an ancient foundation founded by Sir Thomas Gresham in the sixteenth century, who intended it to be a competitor with Oxford and Cambridge. After the Great Fire of London, that plan fell to the ground. The endowment passed to some of the City livery companies, and they used it to sponsor public lectures by allegedly eminent persons in sixteenth-century subjects like rhetoric and physic.

My subject was naturally divinity (now called 'religion,' I believe). The Gresham lectures are indeed given by eminent scholars in their subject who love communicating it to others. My Gresham lectures were on topics of philosophical materialism, the relation of modern science and religion, and the relationship of world religions to each other.

While I was there, the college began to publish these lectures on the internet, and as a consequence they were seen and heard by a worldwide audience. When I am lecturing in other countries, and they list parts of my CV, they often think of my Gresham chair as the most important of all my jobs and are surprised to learn that there are no students or degrees, no extensive campus or students' union. In fact, I have received, and still occasionally receive, letters from China, from people who have used my lectures to learn English. I have to acknowledge, regretfully, that many English people as well as many Chinese people would have no idea of what I am talking about in my lectures. But it is gratifying to think English tourists in China would be able to engage in profound theological conversations with some of their hosts.

Rather to my surprise, in 2009 I was then invited to be a research professor at Heythrop College, a notable Jesuit college in London, then situated in Kensington.

HEYTHROP, 2009-2018

Heythrop was a notable centre for religious education, especially for adults, and it concentrated on philosophy, theology, and psychology. I had been friendly for some years with Frederick Copleston, the author of an outstanding multi-volume history of philosophy, which was much more accurate and less polemical than that of Bertrand Russell. Since he described accurately all the bits of philosophy I knew about, I trusted his judgment, and asked him which of the many views of God he had described so well was the one he accepted. Looking at me quizzically, he said, "I cannot really remember." Nevertheless, there is a more or less standard Catholic view of God, epitomised in Thomas Aquinas. It derives, as almost everything in Thomas does, from Aristotle. These two are both ancient, long-dead philosophers, and though I like many dead philosophers, it seems to me that their work needs a bit of rethinking, even if one is very sympathetic to it.

In particular, as I have already implied, I can see nothing wrong with God changing, and therefore being in a sort of time, though it is obviously not the spacetime of this universe. I think it is positively good that God can respond to prayers in creative ways, and share in the joys and sufferings of creatures. And I think it is good that God can co-operate with the free decisions of finite persons, and relate to them in personal and loving ways, rather than being stuck in the same state, whatever people do or don't do.

It seems to me that Thomists are right in saying, as they do, that God is simple, timeless, and changeless, if that means that God is not made up of simpler elements stuck together, is not confined to our spacetime, and never changes in having the dispositions to understand and love all things. That is logically perfectly compatible with changing responsively in the ways in which God shows understanding and love. In other words, God is changeless and eternal *in nature*, but responsive and relational in the ways God expresses that nature in the world. I cannot see how God could, as

John's Gospel says, 'become' flesh, or intend to include persons in the divine nature, as the second letter of Peter says (2 Peter 1:4), without feeling, responding, and changing in some important respects.

Does this matter? My Catholic colleagues at Heythrop share with me the belief that God was in Christ reconciling the world to the divine self, that Christ died because of human evil, and was raised to assure humans of God's will to enable them to share in the divine nature. Our differences are of a philosophical nature, and they are not conclusively decided by appeal to anything in the Bible. (We all think the Bible supports our view best.) So yes, they matter, but only because they are different ways of understanding the divine wisdom and love, of encountering the demands of love, the power of love, and the promise of love that can be found in Christian discipleship. We just have to live with differences, at least when they seem to be not morally depraved or irrational.

ROEHAMPTON 2018–2020

AT HEYTHROP, WE DID live with differences, in mutual charity and respect. But regrettably, Heythrop College was closed down in 2018. The Jesuits felt that a college with such a small range of subjects was no longer viable, and that their money would be better spent elsewhere. Some of the staff, including me, were then appointed to jobs at Roehampton University, which, surprisingly enough, was in Roehampton, a district of London. I was told I could choose my own title, and I decided to be a professor of the philosophy of religion. This enabled me to complete my own philosophy of religion, and try it out on a set of very lively and religiously diverse students. I think that the general reaction was that I was too religious to be a real philosopher and too unorthodox to be a real theologian. I think that means I just about got it right. As one student put it, even if I did not convince them, I extended their horizons to embrace things they would never otherwise have thought of. And that, perhaps, is what philosophers should do.

I continued to write books, and taught modules on the philosophy of religion for two years. But at the age of eighty-one, the covid pandemic struck, making face-to-face teaching impossible, as people were not allowed to meet in lectures or seminars any more. Luckily, I did not fall victim to the virus, but since it was not possible to teach in person, and since teaching was what I most loved, I decided that I should retire for the third time and make way for some younger teachers. I became fully freelance, continuing to talk to eighteen-year-olds in schools and to take part in various conferences, though I did find it increasingly hard to remember the names of even quite famous people (speaking of which, I now recall that Maurice Wilkins was the 'third man' of DNA). As one famous and forgetful preacher of the past said, "Whenever I said Aristotle, I meant St. Paul." I often had to leave it to students to discover who I was really talking about, but with the aid of Google they usually managed it.

In the years since retiring from Oxford I have written an embarrassingly large number of books, though they all centre on four main themes. I have arranged the books in these themes in what I think is their order of importance. First, there are books about science and religion—*Pascal's Fire* (2006) and *The Big Questions in Science and Religion* (2008)—which argue that modern science, especially cosmology and quantum theory, open up new perspectives for a purposive and value-oriented understanding of the universe.

Second, are books about the nature of religion—*Religion in the Modern World* (2019), *The God Conclusion* (2009), *Morality, Autonomy, and God* (2013), *Why There Is Almost Certainly a God* (2008), *The Evidence for God* (2014), *The Case for Religion* (2004), *Is Religion Dangerous?* (2007), and *Is Religion Irrational?* (2011)– which argue for the importance of religion, as long as it is conducive to a morality of universal justice and compassion, and opposed to violence and censorship of belief. The books also show that most classical philosophers have believed in something very like God, and that modern attacks on the idea of God are mostly based on misunderstandings of both history and of philosophy.

Third, there were books about the Bible—*What the Bible Really Teaches* (2004), *Parables of Time and Eternity* (2021), *The Word of God?* (2010), and *The Philosopher and the Gospels* (2011)—which commend the Bible as a record of the spiritual experiences of the descendants of Abraham, and the inspired, but not infallible, development of an idea of God as the universally wise and unlimitedly loving creator of the cosmos.

Fourth, there were books about Christianity and my own philosophy of personal idealism: *More Than Matter* (2010), *Christianity: A Beginners' Guide* (2008), *Rethinking Christianity* (2007), *Love Is His Meaning* (2017), *The Mystery of Christ* (2018), and *Christianity: A Guide for the Perplexed* (2007). They range from expositions of Christian faith in the modern world to defences of the philosophy of personal idealism.

Then there are five books that form a second attempt at a systematic theology, this time with less emphasis on science and comparative religion, and more on the idea of God as a cosmic Mind who creates a world of emergent self-realising individuals (that includes, but is not limited to, us), whose intended destiny is to achieve final union with the Creator, which thereby realises its own nature as love. This means that human lives, and the universe itself, have a purpose, that we have to work out that purpose ourselves, and that God will realise the divine nature as God includes us in the divine life. These books are: *Christ and the Cosmos* (2015), *The Christian Idea of God* (2017) (I apologise for calling it 'The Christian idea,' since it is only *one* Christian idea, which I happen to accept), and *Sharing in the Divine Nature* (2020), followed by two much shorter books: *My Theology: Personal Idealism* (2021), and *The Priority of Mind* (2021). I think that I would be very pleased if these five books were taken as the final statement of my own philosophy and faith.

Finally (thank goodness, you may well think) there are two semi-autobiographical books, not altogether serious but not altogether false, about what might seem to be my accidental journey into faith, *Confessions of a Recovering Fundamentalist* (2019) and this one. They are meant to be both light-hearted and thought-provoking. Is that possible? That, my dear reader, is for you to judge.

Eudaimonia

MY PHILOSOPHY IN A NUTSHELL

Is this my complete philosophy? Of course it is not really complete, but it is probably just about as far as I am going to get. I call my general philosophical view 'personal idealism'. By this I mean that mind is prior to matter, and that the material universe expresses and realises the nature of a basically mind-like reality. That reality is not 'a person', in anything like a human way, but it is personal, because it is right for us to think of it as knowing, thinking, feeling, and willing, in ways that are analogous to, though very different from, these properties as they are found in humans and other personal finite beings.

What I am most certain about is that truth (understanding and wisdom,) beauty (creativity and appreciation), and goodness (co-operation with and concern for the welfare of others) are the main ideals and demands of any human life. Anything that strengthens them is to be supported, and anything that weakens them is to be eschewed—whether these things are religious or not. (That probably comes from my teaching moral philosophy.)

Then come beliefs about how these ideals fit into a general scheme for understanding the universe. I see them as objective (not just humanly invented) ideals which are inherent in the universe from its beginning. They become purposes for human beings, ideals that humans ought to aim at, each in their own way.

I see humans as emergent self-realising agents who are meant to realise these ideals progressively through time, in an evolutionary universe. (That comes from my teaching philosophy and science.)

Nature necessarily contains possibilities of deviation, of creatively free choices, and of destruction and suffering. Human beings have realised these negative possibilities, and have become alienated from the creative source of life and fulfilment. The deepest human problem is one of overcoming this alienation. (That probably comes from my teaching Hegel and Marx.)

None of these features is necessarily religious. But various religions offer ways of coping with the problem of human alienation. One way, the Abrahamic way, claims to experience God, a cosmic Mind which sets the possibilities and ideals for action, and is also a power for countering negative forces and reinforcing personal endeavours to realise ideals. God has a final goal, which is to realise and hold together a co-operative community of persons united in love. (That comes from my teaching religious studies.)

Springing from the Abrahamic way, Christian faith, a version of which I accept, speaks of Jesus as a man who foreshadows in time this final union of human and divine. His experience was suffused with the sense of the presence of God, and his actions were empowered by the creative energy of God. That is my way of understanding how humanity and divinity were united in him. He gave his life to show the sacrificial nature of divine love, he revealed by the visions of his risen presence the promise of eternal life in God, and he gave to his disciples a share in the power of divine love. In him the demand, the power, and the promise of love was present and manifest. Through him, we might say, the Eternal was unveiled in time, in order that the things of time might share in the life of Eternity. (That comes from my teaching theology.)

This last step is in effect an appeal to a particular revelation, and it reflects back on the very first step, by defining more exactly what I mean by truth, beauty, and goodness. Truth is not just knowing to be true everything that is true. It involves empathetic understanding and practical wisdom. Beauty is not just a Platonic contemplation of a supreme essence of Beauty. It involves the creation and appreciation of beautiful things, the intricate particularities of the world. Goodness is not just a changeless and passionless benevolence. It is involvement in relationships with other persons, in a way that changes each member of the relationship, even when one member is God, for it is in that way that the nature of God as suffering and redemptive love is realised. In this way a particular tradition of revelation reflects back on an initial moral commitment, and the circle of understanding is completed.

This is just one understanding of one way. There are other ways, and there are even other ways of understanding Christian faith, as more conservative Christians are keen to tell me. Insofar as these very different ways seek to establish a morally demanding, rationally intelligible, and personally fulfilling relation to a higher spiritual reality, they have much to offer those who seek the well-being of our world. My belief is that the more we can know and feel the teaching and practice of these ways, the better our spiritual understanding will be. Each of us begins our journey from a particular place with its particular challenges and insights. We can only do our best to respond to these as well as we can.

That is the story of my life. I am sorry that so much of it has taken place inside my own head. I have told the story because, even though my thoughts may seem rather abstract, they have all been heavily influenced by what has been a long, fortunate, and happy life. I dedicate this book to my wife Marian and my two children, Fiona and Alun, with gratitude for their love and patience, and for the ways in which, often unknowingly, they have helped to give me hope for the future of this perplexing world.

80th birthday en famille, 2018

Books by Keith Ward
in Order of Publication

Fifty Key Words in Philosophy. London: Lutterworth, 1968.

Ethics and Christianity. The Muirhead Library of Philosophy. Crows Nest, Australia: Allen and Unwin, 1970.

Kant's View of Ethics. Oxford: Blackwell, 1972.

The Concept of God. Oxford: Blackwell, 1974.

The Divine Image. London: SPCK, 1976.

The Christian Way. London: SPCK, 1976.

The Promise. London: SPCK, 1980. (Revised edition: London: SPCK, 2010.)

Holding Fast to God. London: SPCK, 1982.

Rational Theology and the Creativity of God. Oxford: Blackwell, 1984.

The Living God. London: SPCK, 1984.

The Battle for the Soul. London: Hodder and Stoughton, 1985. (Reissue: *Defending the Soul.* London: Oneworld, 1992, and *In Defence of the Soul.* London: Oneworld, 1998.)

The Turn of the Tide. London: BBC, 1986.

Images of Eternity. London: Darton, Longman, Todd, 1987. (Reissue: *Concepts of God.* London: Oneworld, 1993.)

The Rule of Love. London: DLT, 1989.

Divine Action. London: Collins, 1990. (Reissue: West Conshohocken, PA: Templeton, 2008.)

A Vision to Pursue. London: SCM, 1991.

Religion and Revelation. Comparative Theology, vol. 1. Oxford: Clarendon, 1994.

Religion and Creation. Comparative Theology, vol. 2. Oxford: Clarendon, 1996.

God, Chance, Necessity. London: Oneworld, 1996.

Religion and Human Nature. Comparative Theology, vol. 3. Oxford: Clarendon, 1998.

God, Faith and the New Millennium. London: Oneworld, 1998.

Religion and Community. Comparative Theology, vol. 4. Oxford: Clarendon, 2000.

Christianity: A Short Introduction. London: Oneworld, 2000. (Reissue: *Christianity: A Beginners' Guide*. London: Oneworld, 2008).

God: A Guide for the Perplexed. London: Oneworld, 2002.

What the Bible Really Teaches: A Challenge to Fundamentalists. London: SPCK, 2004.

The Case for Religion. London: Oneworld, 2004.

Pascal's Fire: Scientific Faith and Religious Understanding. London: Oneworld, 2006.

Re-Thinking Christianity. London: Oneworld, 2007.

Is Religion Dangerous? Oxford: Lion, 2007. (New edition with additional chapter on evolutionary psychology, Oxford: Lion, 2010.)

Christianity: A Guide for the Perplexed. London: SPCK, 2007.

Religion and Human Fulfilment. Comparative Theology, vol. 5. London: SCM Press, 2008.

Why There Almost Certainly Is a God. Oxford: Lion, 2008.

The Big Questions in Science and Religion. West Conshohocken, PA: Templeton, 2008.

The God Conclusion. London: DLT, 2009. (American edition: *God and the Philosophers*. Minneapolis: Fortress, 2009.)

More than Matter. Oxford: Lion Hudson, 2010.

The Word of God? The Bible after Modern Scholarship. London: SPCK, 2010.

The Philosopher and the Gospels. Oxford: Lion, 2011.

Is Religion Irrational? Oxford: Lion Hudson, 2011.

God, Autonomy, and Morality. London: Oneworld, 2013.

The Evidence for God. London: DLT, 2014.

Christ and the Cosmos: A Reformulation of Trinitarian Doctrine. Cambridge: Cambridge University Press, 2015.

The Christian Idea of God: A Philosophical Foundation for Faith. Cambridge: Cambridge University Press, 2017.

Love Is His Meaning. London: SPCK, 2017.

The Mystery of Christ. London: SPCK, 2018.

Religion in the Modern World. Cambridge: Cambridge University Press, 2019.

Confessions of a Recovering Fundamentalist. Eugene, OR: Cascade, 2019.

Sharing in the Divine Nature. Eugene, OR: Cascade, 2020.

My Theology: Personal Idealism. London: DLT, 2021.

Parables of Time and Eternity. Eugene, OR: Cascade, 2021.

The Priority of Mind. Eugene, OR: Cascade, 2021.

Ingram Content Group UK Ltd.
Milton Keynes UK
UKHW041822250423
420754UK00004B/276